FRAMING A RAINBOW

How to teach your children to love God

FRAMING A RAINBOW

How to teach your children to love God

JACKINA STARK

College Press Publishing Company, Joplin, Missouri

International Standard Book Number: 0-89900-348-6
Library of Congress Catalog Card Number: 89-81417

Dedicated
to all the dear ones
who have taught me
what love is,
especially to the
Father of Love

Table of Contents

Preface

"Train up a child in the way he should go," the scripture says (Prov. 22:6). I always understood the importance of that verse, but I had no idea just how much delight it would bring.

When I have talked about the joy Tony and I had as we tried to teach our daughters, Stacey Ann and Toni Leanne, what we knew (one of my definitions of parenting), I'm often asked to write it down. So I decided to try.

Ultimately, it seems as though everything we wanted to teach them about life could be subordinated into two major areas: we wanted to show them how much we love them, and we wanted to teach them what we know about God. We felt that if we could do at least these things before it was time for them to go, they would be equipped not only to cope with the world in which they live, but to enjoy it, and even to bless it.

Our story has ended up sounding pretty nice. And it was. But the truth is we could have done much better. Sometimes I do wish I had been more energetic, more wise, more spiritual, more wonderful in general. But we did pass on almost all we knew, and for that, when time was so quickly up, I was glad.

So here I sit, framing a rainbow, the lovely rainbow of our time together. I got that phrase from Lois Elliott Morse's lovely poem, "Memories." After I read it, I decided it was the perfect thing to put at the end of a journal I kept for the girls during their high school years. The speaker in "Memories" is filled with grief because she is afraid tomorrow could never be as wonderful as today. At the close of the poem, God, standing "at the end of the hallway that formed the art gallery" of her life, reassures her that He has more pictures than she could possibly frame. " 'Come,' He beckoned, 'We've only just begun.' "

I found that image very comforting and thought the girls would, too. But even though all four of us will have many more pictures, or rainbows, to frame, I must say, this one was priceless.

Part One

**Showing our children
how much we love them**

Chapter One

"My Heart Hurts"

The day I left both our girls in their college dorm room, I came home, looked at the rooms they had left behind and then sat down on the sofa to try to grasp such an event. I looked up at a large wall portrait of them we'd gotten only the day before. In it they are leaning against a tree, looking off into the horizon. Stacey has her head resting on Leanne's shoulder as the sun breaks through the clouds and shines on them both. It seemed symbolic.

The thunder that began to rumble outside seemed symbolic, too. So did black clouds and the wind and the sheets of rain that beat against the windows. Tony was out, and I was half glad. I cried in peace and thought it quite decent that nature mourned with me.

I also thought it decent that the storm was brief and that in just forty-five minutes or so the sun was shining in its full August force. I decided that was symbolic, too. I thanked God for all the symbolism.

Of course, forty-five minutes would never do for the kind of mourning I would find appropriate for such a passage. But it may have been adequate since I had gone through the bulk of my mourning the year before when Stacey left home for college while Leanne finished her last year of high school.

Actually, I had even started preparing for all this trauma long before that. On a Sunday morning two or three years before when the four of us were riding to church, I told Tony and the girls that because I was so happy, I wanted this moment to stand still. But I knew that wasn't about to happen; I knew life would rush on, as it always does when it is so lovely. I explained that it seemed like I was in a room with the walls closing in on me (remembering Chewy in *Star Wars* somehow robbed the moment of its poignancy).

But the day Stacey left, the mourning began in earnest. When we had gotten Stacey moved in, she hugged and kissed Leanne and me and asked if we would mind if she went with some of her friends. (Shoot no, don't mind us!) We smiled and told her to have a good time. As we were just about to walk out the door, Leanne decided she wanted to leave Stacey a note. She was a chip-off-the-ol'-block; I had already given Stacey a note and a little gift.

This all seemed worse because Leanne hurt as badly as I did. Stacey had been Leanne's best friend since Stacey, at nineteen months, returned from her grandparents' house, pranced into our living room, looked in the bassinet at her three-day-old sister and said, "What's dat?" Now seventeen years later, Leanne finished her note and placed it on Stacey's desk: "Why couldn't I have been the oldest?"

I'm not sure how we got home or which of us drove. Tony was a little scared when he saw us. He had not seen quite so much emotion since Stacey's dog Lady died, and he hardly knew what to do in the face of it. I call Tony my Ecclesiastes man, because for him it is true that there is a time to be born and a time to die, a time to stay home and a time to leave. He really could not understand us.

How could I explain to Tony and any others who could not fathom the difficulty of this situation?

It wasn't that I didn't know that the next stage of my life would be, or could be, as wonderful as this last stage. No telling what Tony and I would do now that our responsibility had decreased so dramatically. In fact, I told a friend that until the girls left, I had never realized what a commitment we had made to them. Yes, I knew I would love all the times of my life. I was that sane, that positive. It was not that I doubted the future; it was that I had loved the past. I was aware of the this-will-never-come-again aspect of it, and I would simply have to have some time to adjust.

Knowing how hard it had been to let Stacey go, Leanne and I were both aware all of her senior year that soon she, too, would leave. One evening I sat typing at my desk in the study while she read on the love seat across the room. I happened to look around at her as she looked over at me. Our eyes connected, and our hearts, too. We knew that moments like these would soon have to be put away. It was difficult. Our "hearts hurt."

Stacey had coined that phrase the summer after her senior year. The three of us were together at Highschoolers on Campus, a camp hosted by the college where I teach. We had been going there together since before they were old enough to go, because I was a dean and took them with me. Those were weeks of great spiritual growth and renewal and fun weeks of special companionship for us. So we all dreaded the last Friday night. Each evening everyone in the camp got together for Koinonia, an hour when the campers sing praise choruses, give "testimonies," or say anything they want to say to one another.

Neither one of the girls had spoken during this time through the years, but on this last Friday night, Leanne got up and told how much these years had meant to us and encouraged the other campers to let their brothers and sisters know how much they loved them, because it wouldn't be long before their time together would be over. When she finished, Koinonia was over and the different "families" (groups of campers put together for the week) went for their final prayer time before lights out. Leanne didn't go with her family; she was too upset. Instead, she found me, and we just sat alone in the chapel and held each other. Finally, we braved walking out into the night. As we were about to go down the hill to our dorm, we looked up and saw Stacey racing toward us. Stacey, who doesn't express herself so easily, grabbed Leanne, threw her arms around her, and pressed her face into her shoulder. Girlhood was almost over, and so was one of the most special experiences that had gone along with it. That's when she said it. Through her tears, she choked out: "My heart hurts."

We used that phrase several times in that passage year. I used it again the day I sat on the sofa after I had left them both. Sitting there, I remembered a day when Stacey was a senior and Leanne a junior. They had just walked out the door to do some shopping. I stood in the living room putting a record on the stereo and heard their busy voices outside, as they headed for the car. Then, as they left and the music started, the strangest phenomena occurred. I half-turned around, but stopped because as the music played in the background, I "heard" their voices in the other room, their eight and nine-year-old voices. That quickly passed, and as I stood there, I heard their voices again, talking and laughing, only this time they were older, eleven and twelve maybe. I don't know how I ever moved.

The other day in a meeting, because it was the Thanksgiving season, we were asked to write a thank you on a little note card we were given. I wrote mine to give to the girls:

I have known a little bit this semester of how quiet our house will

16

be when you aren't there. I thank you for the noise you have filled it with — singing, laughing, hollering — all the lovely noise. I shall hear your voices for always as I walk through our rooms, and I shall always be grateful for them.

Chapter Two

"I Loved You Before You Were Born"

I suppose tucking the girls in each night was consistently the best time of day for the three of us. It was a wonderful time to tell them we loved them; it was a time we all counted on. For us there was never a plan — it just happened. Often it was as simple as getting their favorite blanket out of the closet; pulling all the covers up under their chins; listening to or saying a prayer or a blessing; kissing their faces in four or five good spots; in Leanne's case, scratching her back "good" and making sure her closet doors were closed; and finally before leaving their rooms, looking into their beautiful eyes and saying, "I love you."

Sometimes tucking them in involved hearing highlights of their day. Occasionally there would be a sad story, but most often they made me laugh, and we loved it. During one of Leanne's particularly funny stories, she made me laugh so hard I nearly fell off her bed. Another night early in her eighth grade year, the topic of discussion as I tucked her in was an upcoming, "boring" biography she had to write for one of her classes. As I lay beside her, we began to write the rought draft in our minds. We thought it might make it more interesting to tell her bad points as well as her good ones and mention her hypochondria. Stacey heard us laughing and came in to help us "write." We started with that day's particular malady, a broken nose, and continued this way: "I always hurt — I've had a broken foot; swollen ankles; weak, aching knees; a spastic stomach; bruised ribs; tingly arms; a sore throat; painful, throbbing eardrums, and an annoying brain tumor — all of which are accompanied by permanent nausea and dizziness." Before I turned out the light that night, we had concluded that when Leanne goes to be with the Lord, she should plagiarize an epitaph we once heard: "I told you I was sick!"

Sometimes it involved the three of us piled onto the bed and their listening to me weave great tales from their dad's past or mine: a favorite genre was the Uncle Lance (or Fat Boy, as he gave them permission to call him on a bike ride once) stories. They loved hearing how my younger sister Loren and I had survived life with our "baby" brother. One of their favorites was Lance as a child of seven or eight answering the phone when he really wasn't old enough for such responsibility. He would do anything to beat Loren and me to the phone. One afternoon while he was in the living room playing, commentating and, therefore, saving some imaginary ballgame, the phone rang. Loren and I headed for it, but Lance beat us, smirking as he picked up the receiver. Loren and I watched as he listened importantly and then, in a lower-than-usual voice, called Dad to the phone. Lance had heard Dad talk about Dodson, a very important official on the railroad, and as Dad approached, Lance said, "I believe it's Dodson, Dad." My dad didn't crack a smile as he took the receiver and said, "I hope not, Son, Dodson's been dead for two years." Lance likes to call that story historical fiction, but it's reliable biography from start to finish.

Sometimes I made stories up for them, like the Ben the Bear stories. Even though these stories were generally didactic (stories are a great way to impart truth), the girls enjoyed them because they liked good-natured Ben and they liked the fact that he had two friends, little girls with names amazingly much like theirs: Racey Dan and Soni Peanne. Usually the stories took place in the forest by the little girls' cottage, but in one story the girls took Ben skating with them. That was probably their favorite.

Sometimes I became an imaginary cranky lady from England, named Emily. She was a spin-off of my own mom's imaginary Emily, a tiny English lady who perched on a ceiling light fixture and talked to us, through Mom. My girls always wanted to talk to Emily even though she made it clear she wasn't very fond of children.

Sometimes I became "Granny." She was a lot more fun than Emily, so, naturally, the girls really liked her, too. I did Granny a lot, because her voice was very easy for me. You never knew what Granny was going to do, which was really quite extraordinary, because my imaginary granny was well over one hundred. One night Granny got especially crazy, and I was just glad it was a weekend and that Tony was still coaching and out of town. The girls were just about to get into bed when Granny did something she had never done before; she jumped onto their bed and continued to jump as if she were on a trampoline. As she jumped, she said something like, "Look, Girls, watch Granny jump. You can still jump when you're old, you know." The girls were laughing hysterically to see such an "old" woman jumping on their bed. Jumping really high. Then, the worst scenario possible — Granny fell. The girls ran to help her and were enormously relieved to hear her still talking: "I think Granny's legs are broken, Girls. Oh well, don't worry. Grannies

21

can get along just fine with broken legs." The girls really admired that.

Sometimes tucking them in involved reading a story. I wonder how many times I read "Up in the sky in the shape of a V — how many wild geese can you see?" How many times did we ask, *"Marvin K. Mooney, Will You Please Go Now"?* I wish I had read Gladys Hunt's *Honey for a Child's Heart* when the girls were young, and I would have read more often than I did. In one chapter she paraphrases from Erich Fromm's *The Art of Loving*: a child needs both milk and honey from his parents. "Milk is the symbol of the care a child receives for his physical needs, for his person. Honey symbolizes the sweetness of life, that special quality that gives the sparkle within a person." Fromm says that most mothers are capable of giving milk, but only a very few can give honey. Hunt adds that "to give honey, one must love honey and have it to give. Good books are rich in honey." She reminds parents that books can expose children to grand things and create a desire for those things in their lives, things like determination, courage, mercy, compassion, and loyalty. "A young child, a fresh uncluttered mind, a world before him — to what treasures will you lead him? With what will you furnish his spirit?"

I remember lying between the girls one evening furnishing their spirits with nobility, selflessness, and love. We were reading *The Lion, the Witch, and the Wardrobe* and were into the chapter where the good lion Aslan gives his life to save one of the erring little boys. We could hardly read for crying. Aslan, a symbol of Jesus, captures the hearts of children and the hearts of those who can be childlike. The night a good friend of ours, a father of three, was reading this particular chapter to his children, he had to ask his two boys who Aslan represented so they could realize what would happen to the slain Aslan in the next chapter. Until he reminded them of that, they would not let him put the book down and put them into bed. A book is a nice way to end a day.

Sometimes we had very serious conversations at bedtime. One time when Leanne was a junior in high school she had a friend spend the night. When I tucked both her and her friend in, for some reason we started talking about marriage. After about twenty minutes or so, Leanne fell asleep, and her friend and I talked for quite a while longer. The next day Leanne told her friend she fell asleep because she was so tired, plus she and I had talked about all that many times before. Her friend said she and her mom never talked about marriage. I was amazed. That seemed to me to be one of the most important things we would talk to our children about. Leanne thought it was, too, but she was not surprised like I was: "Mom, my friends' mothers don't talk to them about those kinds of things."

We had serious bedtime conversations from the time they were very young. They weren't very old at all when I told them about loving them before they were born. Children can understand significant ideas, and they listened closely when I told them about my choosing their father to marry. I explained that I married him for many good reasons. (Actually this was their first marriage talk, and they didn't even know it.) I wanted a man with certain qualities that I found admirable and qualities that would complement mine. But, most of all, I wanted a man who would be a good father to the children I thought I would some day have. That was honestly part of my decision, and I wanted them to know that I loved them that much, even before they were conceived.

I tried to explain to them how I felt when I found out my dream of them had become reality. I showed them a poem I had sent my parents to tell them I was carrying my first child. I found it in some material at the doctor's office and adopted it for myself, because someone had written exactly what I felt:

Sweetness pervades my being today
Life holds beauty, death no terror.
Another day may bring
Pain, clouds, tears,

But today, God is nearer, family dearer,
With dignity I bear myself
As one on whom great honor is bestowed.
For today, none other than God,
Creator of this mysterious universe,
Provider of planets
Sustainer of life—
Has deigned to call me partner
In creation
I am with child.

I have no pain tolerance. None. But I would have paid Tony good money to let me be the one to waddle when I walked, to need help rolling over in the middle of the night and to have my body ripped apart giving birth to those babies. The experience was that magnificent.

The morning Stacey was put into my waiting arms for the first time, I thought I would not be able to contain my joy. I honestly felt I would burst if I could not release it. So when a nurse took my baby back to the nursery, I asked my mom to get me a pencil and some paper so that I could write down how I felt. Although trying to express how I felt pacified me enough that I could rest when I had finished, what I wrote did not begin to explain the love I felt for that child.

And that's something I was not willing to keep to myself. I wanted the girls to know how boundless our love is. It is something like, but not quite as vast as, God's love for them.

Chapter Three

"You Delight Me!"

I started what I now call the "Baby Journal" when Stacey was nine months old. It was something I almost had to do. In the first entry of that journal, I explained that I wrote so that I would "never forget." Never forget the image, no matter how common, and never forget how it made me feel. My first line was "I had to write today so that I may always remember how happy I am right now. Stacey Ann is the sweetest thing. I am thrilled that she is mine." Then I told about the ordinary event that had generated all this emotion. Beans. As I sat at the kitchen table separating beans, Stacey sat in her walker, running herself around the slick kitchen floor. Every time the beans "hit the bowl Stacey burst out laughing" — the kind of baby laughter that goes on and on, giggle after giggle, until the baby nearly collapses with exhaustion. It was so enchanting that I'd only give her a minute to rest before I would throw some more in; they'd clang, and she'd start backing up in her walker, laughing hysterically all over again.

I kept that journal fairly regularly for two or three years. Then as life got more and more hectic, I wrote less and less often, until I finally put it away. I almost forgot it.

Until the night of the blizzard, three or four years later. That night I found it and came to know, quite by accident, just how much it means to children, even children as young as seven and eight, to know they are loved and adored.

The girls, just in the second and third grades, were totally unaware of the journal, and I had no idea if they would be interested in it. I was surprised at just how fascinated they were to read about when they were babies. They wanted to read every word. This night had to be as idyllic as we ever got. The snow fell in huge flakes outside the kitchen window while a mother sat at the table in her warm kitchen holding her girls on her lap, three heads bent over a hand-written journal that chronicled their beginnings.

Their amusing beginnings, for the most part. We read about Tony's walking into Stacey's bedroom to find her rubbing Vaseline all over her horse's bottom. She must have watched me change Leanne for months and decided she was taking no more chances: her horse wasn't about to get diaper rash. We "laughed our heads off."

Except when we came to the entry of March 7, 1972. Then, to balance cliches, we "cried our eyes out." I couldn't believe it. I didn't think I could finish reading the entry or that the girls would be able to finish listening. It didn't matter that the entry was a bit corny and needed revision. It's as though they saw straight into the heart of this very young woman, a woman who felt so inadequate at times, as she wrote to little girls who were only three and almost two at the time:

Should my children ever have occasion to read this, let me say that you are my beloveds. You have brought me a joy that will last forever, no matter what happens from this time forth. I pray to God for your happiness and pray you'll always find strength in Jesus Christ, and then I worry not. How I love you! At this time in my life I am a selfish person and not as giving as I should be, but know this — I love you with a love that almost bursts my heart. I hope that in your lives you won't betray your dad or me, or God, but most of all, yourselves. Be strong girls, and be girls that go with "the abiding peace" in their hearts.

I just held them after I finished reading and knew I had learned something very important: Tony and I must not pass up chances to let the girls know, by what we do and by what we say, how much we love them.

That's one of the reasons why I decided to keep their high school journal. I'll always believe the thought came from God. For years, I had been trying to think of something special I could give the girls — something I could make. I couldn't quilt, cross stitch, knit, paint, or sew. Nothing. But just when I was about to give up, and just when I least expected it, the idea came. I was tossing and turning one night all alone in my bed, because Tony was in Kansas City attending a meeting. As I lay there trying to sleep, I slipped into prayer for the girls. And that's the exact moment the idea came: I could keep a secret journal of their high school years. It was a great idea. After all, the girls had loved their baby journal, and I could gather information easily enough since they were so naturally open and talkative. In addition, the timing was perfect. It was September of Stacey's first year of high school, and Leanne was just one year behind her. I would save for them some of the things that are inevitably lost: where they went, what they said, why they laughed and cried. I would record any significant event and as many ordinary ones as I could. I would record my prayers for them. Thanks, Father, for a perfect "Project." So excited I couldn't sleep, I got up, put on my robe, and went downstairs to begin. I wrote a preface that I decided would end this way: "Five years. Well, my Loves, here it is. The PROJECT. It is my labor of love, like a quilt or album. My gift is words. And they all mean — I LOVE YOU."

This would be something I would give them when it was time for them to go, and it would be one more time, one more way, to tell them how much they blessed us.

I don't like to blame God for everything, but I think it might not have been an accident that I was asked to speak in Hawaii the last month that I kept the journal, just a week or two before Leanne's graduation. I would never have dreamed I could take the girls on such a trip; we just didn't have that kind of imagination or money. But we did go and had eight beautiful days together to fill with memories — things like getting lost walking from the Hard Rock Cafe back to our modest accommodations, or like Stacey and I nearly choking to death from laughing under water while snorkling at Hanauma Bay. One evening a dear lady from one of the churches there took us to dinner. She commented to me that she enjoyed us so much because she hadn't been around young, beautiful girls who could go somewhere like Hawaii and have fun doing everything with their mother. She thought they were quite extraordinary. Naturally, the first thing I did when we got back to the hotel was tell them someone thought they were extraordinary.

I'm sure I didn't seize every opportunity to let the girls know they were loved and special; I was much too tired and distracted for that, but I seized a bunch of them. Like the time I ran into something of a self-possessed feminist while visiting a student at the hospital. As we chatted in the room, she asked me how I felt about my children. I could not pass up the chance to tell my junior high girls what I had told her. Trying to put how I felt into words had been hard. But I ended up saying what I meant in a remarkably few words: "They delight me!" We've used that phrase a lot since then.

We used it the night of Leanne's graduation. Tony and I had

just gone to bed when we heard noises in the attic. Leanne, with Stacey's help, was looking for something she had written a year or two before, which she had saved to give to us on just such an occasion. When she finally located it, she and Stacey plopped on our bed and handed us our letter. It was a reversal of a snowy night ten years before. This time I read words she had written: "I'm glad I got born into this family. You're my beloveds. You delight me."

With her sense of comic relief, she added that her dad would delight her a lot more if he would let her sleep a little more.

Children who know they are adored and cared for seem to have a great deal of strength, confidence, peace and joy.

Chapter Four

"Then My Heart With Pleasure Fills"

The night I nearly fell out of Leanne's bed laughing, she said, "Mom, I love it when you laugh at me." What she meant was that it made her feel good to know I enjoyed her. They both liked to make me laugh and were experts at it.

When Leanne was in the eighth grade, she fell madly in love with a young man named "Jason." I couldn't blame her; he was quite a nice young man. Leanne, not being a modern girl, refused to pursue him openly, but adored him subtly from afar. For months. We chatted about Jason while driving home from school one day. I'll never know what possessed me to ask such a stupid question when we pulled up to a red light: "Leannie, do you think it bothers Jason that you are a foot taller than he is?"

"Well, if it does . . ." she started. Then she paused briefly, and I, being incredibly in tune with my offspring, automatically finished what I thought would be her answer. I expected her to say, "he'll have to get tough" or "he'll have to get over it." I've taught my girls that philosophy; that's how I knew what she'd say.

But that isn't what she said at all. Instead I heard: "Well, if it does, I'll just have to cut my legs off!"

"Until this moment," I told her when I composed myself enough to talk, "I didn't know what the word devotion meant." That story has now become part of our oral tradition.

I think most children like to hear not only that we love them but also that they charm us, tickle us, delight us. I was reminded of this not long ago while grading journals my writing students kept last semester. One of the young men wrote about getting a letter from his father, a letter so unlike him that he thought it must have been copied. The father wrote to say how proud he was of his son. My student looks like a grown man. He is a grown man. But he absolutely revelled in his father's praise. "I'm so happy," he wrote. He is twenty years old, but when his dad told him of his pleasure in a letter, the student wrote a journal entry about it, ending with, "I will cherish it for the rest of my life."

It makes our children feel good to know how they enhance our lives. I've told the girls they are my identification with Wordsworth's poem, "I Wandered Lonely As a Cloud." The speaker comes over a hill to see the most glorious sight: thousands of dancing daffodils lining the margin of a bay. Forever afterwards when he was resting in "vacant or in pensive mood," he would remember that image. "Then," says the speaker, "my heart with pleasure fills, and dances with the daffodils."

I must have hundreds of pictures to call up when I am in "vacant or pensive mood." One in particular I recorded in their journal. They were outside with their father doing their least favorite job: mowing the yard. When they got into their teens, they wanted to mow with a sack on their heads. They said something about being the only kids they knew who had to do such a thing. Tony never had a new lawnmower, but he always had a lot of them. At least three. (The girls say there were four, but I just refused to use mine.) One day the grass was so high that we had to mow it even if a storm was forecast. As it always happened when Tony made lawn-mowing noises, I found work inside. If I didn't have a load of wash to do, I pulled clean clothes off hangers to create a somewhat acceptable excuse. As I walked by an upstairs window with my customary load of wash, I heard and saw what would become for me a classic memory. All three of them were pushing lawnmowers on our sizeable front lawn. Then I noticed the sky had become dark. I heard the thunder and at the same time, Tony's voice instructing the girls to "hurry — the storm's coming." They beat the storm, and it was a race I shall never forget. There I stood looking down on a determined man and his two tiny, driven daughters running those old lawn mowers frantically back and forth down parallel paths. The only thing that would have been funnier is if they had had those sacks on their heads. Yes, "then my heart with pleasure fills, and dances with the daffodils!"

They liked knowing they entertained us, but they also liked knowing they made us proud. When Stacey got the top student award at her junior high awards assembly, we brought that horrible plaque home and hung it in the hall, even if the shiny red (yes, red) plate was crooked and the wrong year was engraved on it. It's a good thing we did, too, because although the girls did well in school, we never had a top student award to hang again, red or otherwise.

Tony and I were plenty proud that day, but one of my proudest moments was when they came home from camp one year and had won best camper and runner up. My cup really ran over, however, when I heard what happened. Everyone stood outside to hear the winners announced. When they called

Stacey's name for runner-up, Leanne went slightly wild, jumping up and down and yelling, "Alright, Stacey!" The youth minister telling me the story said that while she was still in mid-air, rejoicing for Stacey, they called out Leanne's name for best-camper. I was glad to know someone thought they were acting well, even when I wasn't around. But I was especially glad to see that the girls had learned to praise each other and be happy for one another. That makes life so good.

Letting them know we appreciated so many things about them is probably what psychology books would call positive reinforcement. Stacey did something when she was about twenty months old that she has heard me tell many times through the years. I have wondered if that played any part in her charming tendency toward gratitude.

She was just a tiny nineteen pounds when she lay in that hospital bed recovering from a very serious operation. She was quite a sight with feeding tubes in her neck and foot and another tube inserted in her nose and pushed down into her stomach to prevent vomiting. Her arms had been put on splints to keep her from pulling any of the tubes out by accident or on purpose. But as miserable as she looked and must have been, she was such a pleasant thing. The nurses adored taking care of her. After Stacey had been in the hospital several days, my sister came from out of town to visit her and, naturally, to bring her a gift. She brought a clear ball that had a merry-go-round inside. Our horse-lover could not believe her eyes. She gasped audibly. Then she took the ball with her stiff, splinted arms and held it out straight up in front of her and said, "Oh, tank you!" Everyone in the room melted. My sister rushed out of the room to go by out Wal-Mart.

I always appreciate a thankful heart. I can't imagine the poverty of one who cannot be grateful. The girls were so much fun to buy for or do for, because they always said thank you and seemed to truly mean it. They didn't always get everything they wanted and were happy anyway. When the girls had special functions to attend, sometimes they got new dresses, but sometimes they didn't. On one occasion when Stacey needed something dressy, she was content to wear one of my dresses. It made me so happy to know she could make do with that. On another occasion when we didn't buy her a new dress, she amazed me when she spent the afternoon at the mall helping a friend pick out her new dress. She came home and told me all about it, without a trace of envy. I was so happy to see that attitude. I knew it would serve her well.

My heart was filling to the brim with pleasure again. And again, I thought to tell her.

Chapter Five

"Let Me Lay Here Just a Minute"

The Stark Family had gathered together for some holiday or other, and a very important game was being played at the kitchen table. My partner, a very serious player, was my father-in-law; our almost-worthy opponents were Tony and one of his brothers, either Jerry or Bobby the cut-throat. Leanne, who was around a year and a half at the time and bored with her sister and cousins, came in and asked me if I'd hold her — "for just a minute." After about fifteen of them had passed, I told Leanne she'd better hop down and go into the other room to play with the other kids. She snuggled in a little closer. After several more minutes, I told her again. Then Tony told her. We both told her. She was determined to stay, for a lap was her favorite place to be, especially mine. After too many kind, reasonable requests, Tony made his last request with an especially firm voice and moved toward her somewhat threateningly. At this time, Leanne grudgingly slid off my lap and grumbled as she walked past us out of the room: "OK, if you don't love your little chillens . . . ."

Leanne was born wanting to be held.

When she was just a little over two, she spent the night with her Granny Stark. Mr. Stark had died not very long before, and her granny was so glad to have her there. Snuggling her close while rocking her, she said, "Leanne, I just wish you could stay here with your granny!" She made her granny laugh when she sat straight up, turned around and looked at her very seriously and said, "Now, Granny, I can come *visit* you, but I cannot live with you; I am not your child."

If I hadn't held her as often as I did, she might not have been so adamant.

My office-mate Rex Wolfe says God blesses children and fools, and it must be true. For I was pretty immature when the girls were born, yet things went well with them. My mom made the comment when they were babies that I just seemed to be a "natural" mom. I appreciated that. I couldn't imagine how that could be, but I sort of knew what she meant. I think it was the enjoyment factor. One of the most important things I did, and it did come naturally, was hug them, hold them, and kiss them. They basked in the security of that. Especially Leanne.

Now, to be sure, Stacey liked the closeness of a hug and a kiss. My goodness, even as a sophomore in college, twenty years old, she likes me to kiss her goodnight and goodbye, or for no reason at all. It is not unusual for her to come over to be held briefly while we and any number of other people are visiting in the kitchen. But Leanne falls into another category altogether. I'm sorry to say we had to call her Leanne Leech.

She has always needed to be touched. I think lots of people inherently need that. Studies show that there is a difference between children who receive that kind of nurturing and those who don't. Now that she's eighteen, things haven't changed a whole lot. I praise God that the sweet, God-loving man she will marry this summer likes to hug and hold. That was one of my major requests when I prayed for a husband for her. She really does have a minimum daily requirement.

I know some people would be appalled to know that although she started the night in her own bed, at some point almost every night she would crawl into bed with us. It started when she could barely walk. She started walking before she was ten months old. She didn't care that she couldn't; she just kept trying until she finally did. And as soon as she could do it fairly successfully, she started figuring out how to get out of her baby bed so that she could pad down the hall to where her mom and dad lay in their warm, wonderful bed. She would crawl up, pat my face, snuggle in beside me and say, "Let me lay here — just a minute."

"Lie here," I corrected. Just kidding. Actually, I didn't say anything. I just pulled her close, kissed her forehead and fell back asleep.

When she was about two and a half, we became concerned. Maybe we were letting her become too dependent on us. Maybe we ought to bring this habit to a halt while we still could.

So we set the date for our deliverance. When we put Leanne to bed, we told her that it was time for her to sleep in her own bed. All night. "Watch Stacey," we quipped. She seemed to understand. We had no idea a marathon nightmare was about to begin.

I don't know how long Tony and I had been asleep before she came in the first time. I woke myself up and reminded her of the deal. Then I very calmly took her back to her bed. I kissed her, probably reassured her that I knew this wasn't easy, but that she could do it. I'm sure I left saying it would be morning before we knew it.

Not by a long shot, I was soon to learn.

It might have been a half-hour later when I realized Tony

and I had company again. I remained calm. It was not much past midnight yet. There was no sense calling this an ordeal. I picked her up once more and took her back to her bed. We talked through the plan once more. This time I threatened her. Maybe that is what was needed. Well, I had said it would not be easy.

So when she came to our bed an hour or so later, I took her back to her room and smacked her sweet little legs and told her with a firm voice that she *would* sleep in her bed. I tried to feel right about it; after all, this was for her own good.

When she returned a fourth time, I was not calm. I took her back to bed and smacked her again. I didn't like it then, and I don't like it now, but I reasoned that perhaps nothing else would work. I told her not to get back in our bed and marched out of her room. When I crawled back into bed, I made my hourly report to Tony's sleeping back, a back that had to get up and go to work in a few hours. We were unhappy.

I don't know how much time had passed when I sensed a presence. I was aware of someone or something before I was even conscious and before I opened my eyes. Lying on my side, looking toward the wall, I slowly opened my eyes. There she stood. Right by my pillow, just staring at me, but very obviously not touching the bed. When my eyes focused on her face, she bent over, still careful not to touch that bed, and kissed my cheek. I closed my eyes. I was exhausted. When I opened them again, she still stood there, like a baby sentry. Then she bent over once more and kissed my cheek.

I gave up and pulled my arm out of the warm blankets and pulled a little baby girl, who needed human contact, close beside me. She stayed there until she was ready to go back to her bed. We did not break her habit that night. In fact, it was several years before she was ready to stay in her bed all night.

At the time I had not had any psychology courses, but I decided that all children need the human touch, and some need a good deal of it. Immature or not, I had the intuition to show them, with a lot of physical contact, they were loved.

I think I saw some of the fruits of that the night I was recovering from having my wisdom teeth cut out. I was fairly miserable and very intent on not disturbing blood clots and getting those dreaded dry sockets I had heard about. But that would be a problem, because Tony had a ball game out of town, and I had first- and second-grade daughters to get ready for bed. All evening while I lay flat on the couch, the girls had played quietly. When their bedtime rolled around, I started contemplating rising and taking care of my responsibilities. (I would have been a great pioneer.) Just when I had worked up my courage to begin, they appeared. They were dressed in their pajamas and had come to tell *me* goodnight. They had no intention of letting their suffering mother get up. Before they left to put themselves in bed, they tenderly covered me up with a blanket, kissed me goodnight and told me that they loved me. When I heard them safely in bed, I lay there sort of in disbelief. Ordinarily I would have cried at such sweetness, but I was too awed.

They both have a part-time job now while they attend college. They have chosen to work at a day-care center. It amazes me to hear them talk about "their" kids. They just love them. But working there hurts, too. It hurts them to see some children, only three or four, who are angry. They say some of them have every reason to be angry. One of the little boys runs up to hug his mother when she arrives, and the girls die a little to watch her literally push him away and say, "Don't touch me; you'll mess up my clothes." I did not believe that could really happen. But it did; they saw it, time and time again. Leanne has the "babies," the two and three year olds. One of them is two-year-old "Ben." He's just one of the reasons she's willing to work the number of hours she does. She makes it a point to hug each child every day and to hold most of them. Sometimes when she's holding another child, Ben comes up to her, holds his arms up and says, "Take," only he says it more like, "Ta-a-a-ke."

Ben has taught us that little boys like to be held, too. Once Leanne saw him making a strange face at her. "What do you want, Ben?" she asked. One word was his reply, "You." As Ben has put it, "You my friend." Every day before Leanne leaves the day-care, all her "babies" line up for a goodbye kiss. She thinks it's important. She's not surprised that they love it.

Chapter Six

"Watch Me Do Tricks"

Tony and I didn't have a lot to do last night, but it's just as well, because Stacey was cheering for Ozark Christian College, and we needed to be there to watch.

I guess this is just as good a time as any to confess. In the first chapter I mentioned my trauma at the girls leaving home for college. I didn't mention that they were moving into a dorm that was no more than eight minutes from home and that I drove right by it nearly every day when I went to that college to teach English. Nor did I mention that this semester I have them both in class.

I didn't mention it because that wasn't the point. Plus, I didn't want to hear anyone laugh. Some people understand, I'm sure. It wasn't that I wouldn't be seeing them. It's that things would never be the same again; it's that I couldn't hear the muffled sounds of their voices as they talked together while taking their makeup off in their bathroom each night; it's that they weren't there to tuck in; it's that we were now living such separate lives when we had been such a unit; it's that this change was a herald for all the others that were on its heels.

Children know they're loved when parents spend time with them. I honestly think that most children don't care how much money is spent on them. Time is a far more precious commodity. One night after I had spent fifteen or twenty minutes rocking Leanne to sleep, I asked her two-year-old sister what I could do for her. As I've mentioned, she didn't need nearly as much touching; she had something else in mind. Her eyes lighted up at my question and her response was swift: "Watch me do tricks!" So for the next fifteen or twenty minutes, I sat watching a little girl tumble and dance and turn, stopping every few minutes to see if her audience was impressed. And I most certainly was.

I'm also impressed with how many friends we have who are such dedicated parents, in that they spend so much time with their children. Some of the mothers work; some do not, but despite a lack of energy and despite other pressing matters to attend to, they are always there for the endless soccer games, football games, basketball games, baseball games, wrestling matches, track meets, piano and dance recitals, and all the school and church programs. Not only do they attend these functions, showing their concern for and pride in their children, but they also spend time with them just doing things as a family, showing their children how pleasant they are to have around.

Not all children have that advantage. Some live the sad life recorded in the classic song, "Cat's in the Cradle." Almost everyone has probably heard the song that starts with a man saying that when his child was born, he had "planes to catch and bills to pay" and his son learned to walk and talk while he was away. In the refrain, the son asks his father when he is coming home, and the father answers, "I don't know when, but we'll get together then — you know we'll have a good time then." Throughout the song the boy says he's going to grow up to be like the daddy he adores. At the end, he does. When the father calls his grown son and asks him to come home for a visit, the son says what the father has told him all his life, and it is clear they will never be together. A whole country seemed to relate to that song.

Earlier I mentioned the journals my students keep. So many students write about their feelings for their parents. Often it is heartwarming; sometimes, heartbreaking. One fellow said he had been on the interstate, traveling back from his girlfriend's house on Thanksgiving, when he heard a song he'd never heard before — "Cat's in the Cradle." Although it was new to him, he summarized it accurately and even quoted parts of it. From what he said, I could tell it was because he identified with it. At the end of his entry, he said, "How true it is." A twenty-year-old college man expressed subtle pain, and once again I knew how important it was that we be together.

Tony had a rule when the girls were in high school that they could not go out nights during the week. There were exceptions to that rule, but they were home often. We didn't care if we didn't have anything special to do or even say on a given night. It somehow mattered that, if we were doing nothing but reading or studying a lesson, that we were together doing it. He was a daddy that went to open houses at school when he really didn't want to; he made the girls do chores with him and taught them responsibility and that he liked their company; he took them places with us, even when they were teens and could have done things with their friends instead. And they seemed so happy. Maybe that's why they won't sing the refrain of "Cat's in the Cradle" to their dad. Instead they bought him the country western tape (even though they hate country/western) with the song "That's My Job" on it. To this day when they listen to that song, tears form in their eyes. At the beginning of it, a little boy walks down the hall during a storm and asks his dad if he can sleep with him. In the refrain of this song, the father says, "That's My Job, that's what I do. Everything I do is because of you, to keep you safe with me; that's my job, you see." The song summarizes their life together, and at the end when the father dies, the son writes this song for him, because that has become his job, "to keep" his father safe with him, through his song.

You never know what an open house or a track meet will mean to your child. We still laugh at how "boring" we are that the four of us could have gone to the girls' high school open house and call that a nice evening. The reason it was labled that is because Tony topped the evening off by taking us to McDonald's. It wasn't such a big night that we went in. No, Tony insisted on zipping through and picking up our hot-fudge sundaes at the drive-through window. It was more special than it sounds, though, because we didn't drive right home. Tony pulled over, and we ate in the parking lot. What a guy; what a night! Strange how "ordinary" is so capable of making memories.

The track meet looked ordinary too, but as I found out yesterday, seven years after the fact, it was not ordinary at all. I have Stacey in my writing class this semester, and when I had the class write an in-class paper the second day to see what they could do, Stacey wrote about her seventh grade track meet. I thought that the only significant things that happened at that track meet were that Stacey's relay team won and that one of her teammates said Stacey's mom was pretty. But Stacey's very well-done paper revealed it was much more significant than that: it was a major turning point.

I didn't realize that in the seventh grade she felt like a "dork," but she did. She is quick to reassure me now that she didn't feel like one at home, but at her new junior high school she did. She knew hardly anyone, she was extremely shy at this time in her life, and she had a short hair cut that made her look like a boy. In fact, when she asked for directions to the gym the first day of school at this junior high, the teacher directed her to the boy's gym. This did not help. So there she was — shy, no friends, and looking like a boy. But that all changed at the track meet.

She almost didn't try out, but she was a good runner, and she went ahead because of the "encouragement of her family." She was on a relay team with three other girls who had been friends a long time. They weren't mean to Stacey, but they did tend to leave her out. I'll let Stacey's paper take over from here:

So I stretched and jogged and prepared for my race instead of chit-chatting with the rest of them.

When the coach came and told me it was time to go to the starting line, I was ready. We rounded up the other girls and headed for the track. I was so excited.

"Runners to your marks!" shouted the starter. BANG! And they were off. The three other girls on my team were also good runners, but not as good as the ones they were up against. We soon fell behind. But, I hadn't run yet.

As soon as I got the baton, I started running like I had never run before. (Even *I* didn't know I could run that fast!) I passed the first girl in hardly any time at all. There was just one more girl to pass, but she was way ahead of me, and I only had 220 yards to catch her and pass her. From somewhere unknown to me came another burst of incredible energy. I saw myself catch the girl, pass her, and take a sizeable lead to win the race. I had never felt so good in all my life.

When I got back to the stands where the entire track team had watched me save the day, I was a heroine. People who had never looked at me before told me what a great job I had done. The coaches patted me on the back. For that moment, I wasn't a dork, but the coolest person in the world.

Even after everyone realized that I was fast, I was still shy, and I still looked like a boy, but that day was a beginning for me. I began to come out of my shell and just be myself. Gradually the shyness wore off and my hair grew out. Now I'm fairly outgoing, and one can tell of which gender I am. And it all started with an 880 relay.

When I read that, I felt a lot of things; not the least of them was gratitude that I had been there. I'm sorry to say that I was not always there. One of my biggest regrets is missing an out-of-town swim meet the girls were in when they were six and seven. One of my good friends took them. The meet ran very late, and Arla had to wake Leanne up for her to swim her last relay. You just don't know how much I wish I had been holding her so that I could have awakened her and encouraged her. Whatever reason I had for not going was not good enough.

But I was at that track meet. When Stacey looked into the stands, it wasn't just her track team and coaches she saw. She saw her dad and me. We shared her moment, even if we were unaware we had witnessed more than a simple victory. This day was not unlike the day she was so pleased that I had watched her do tricks.

Chapter Seven

"I Knew You Were Going to Say That"

Something all of us enjoyed was being "on the road" together. In town or out.

Even going from one place to another in town could be an adventure. I dreaded their driving not because I worried about them; they are better drivers than I. No, I dreaded it because we didn't have nearly as many occasions to be in the car together, and that had been a great deal of fun.

Sometimes it didn't seem like fun except in retrospect. Once when I picked them up after their piano lessons, I got our car caught on top of a low brick wall that lines the driveway. The girls hid in the back seat until I made them get out and help lift the car off that wall so that we could get away from there and try to restore our dignity. Where were those sacks?

Of course, that wasn't half as bad as the day we had my mom in the car with us and were crossing a large and busy intersection. As I sat at the stop sign, Mom looked over at the gas gauge and warned me that my vehicle was running precariously low on fuel. I assured her there was a filling station only three or four blocks away. From the back seat, Leanne suggested I pull over and walk to the station for gas. But before I could really give her suggestion much thought, traffic cleared, and I went for it. I probably didn't get two feet before the car coughed to a stop. I felt really bad. I felt even worse that it was necessary that I steer the car while the others pushed. Justice was not done that day, as I peered into my rearview mirror and cracked up watching my mother and her two little granddaughters pushing my car across those four lanes to safety. I decided we needed a supply of sacks for the backseat of the car.

You never knew what would happen when I chauffeured. Once Leanne pointed out something on my left, I looked, and we crashed. None of us was hurt, but Stacey almost suffered heart failure because we had just pulled away from the McDonald's drive-through, and the Big Mac that she had not taken "one bite out of" landed, astonishingly enough, on my visor. Her fries landed on the floor at her feet but were at least within reach. She crammed several into her mouth before I noticed.

We couldn't always count on adventure, but we could count on good conversation. The car is one of the best places in the whole world to talk. One Halloween when they were in junior high, we started discussing the ghost of Halloweens Past as we headed home after dropping off one of their friends. How I wish that in those days there had been the present awareness many Christians now have about the "dangers" of Halloween. It would have let me off the hook. Halloween had been an ordeal for me. I felt so handicapped. I couldn't sew; I was always the proverbial day late and dollar short to have an exciting costume made; and I wasn't creative enough to dredge up a decent costume from things that might have lurked around the house. Some Halloweens weren't so bad. A kind soul gave them costumes when they were in the first and second grades. Leanne was an adorable bee. I wish that were the only costume she remembered.

As we drove home this day, I realized all wishes don't come true. For she remembered the fourth grade. Yes, she contrasted greatly with a sweet little girl we knew who went proudly to her costume party dressed as the cluster of grapes the spies brought back from the valley of Eschol. Thank goodness she went to a different school. Leanne showed up at her school as a headless horseman, which sounds much better than it was. I took a shirt and buttoned it up over Leanne's head, finding a way for her to peek out (she had to be able to see to play games). Maybe she would have forgotten if I had stopped there. But it just didn't seem like enough. So I got a plastic pumpkin with a face on it that we had sitting around and had her carry that under her right arm. That was sort of a twist, the headless horseman carrying his head. Even that was forgivable. But then I gave her a bottle of aspirin (almost empty and with a child-proof lid, of course) and told her to carry that in her left hand and to say when she saw people, "Oh goodness! I've got *such* a headache." I think I might have been kidding, but if I were, she did not know it. So being an obedient child, she did that all day long. Games must have been a nightmare with a pumpkin in one hand and an aspirin bottle in the other. Riding home and talking about it several Halloweens later, we laughed so much I'm surprised we didn't have another wreck.

You wouldn't think there would be time for all that just driving from one point to another in town, but there is. There's time for a lot of things. In fact, one Saturday afternoon when I was taking them to meet friends at the mall, they told me a story that affected me so much that I pulled the car over to the side of the road and cried.

They told me about a *That's Incredible* segment they had

51

seen the night before with their dad. The parents of a boy diagnosed as hopelessly retarded were advised to put their son in an institution. The parents refused, and in this case, the love of parents nurtured even such a severely handicapped child. When the boy's mother died in 1979, his father took full responsibility for him — dressing him, giving him his shots, and helping him with the smallest tasks such as crossing the street. But that wasn't what was incredible. What was incredible was his one, and only one great ability — to paint. Despite the fact that he was born with cataracts inside both eyes, blocking the light and causing him to paint just a few inches from the table, he paints enough and well enough to have had eight one-man shows in one year alone! Some artists don't accomplish this in a lifetime. It takes him only three hours for a small picture and two, three or four days for larger ones. He is unbelievable at details and can remember and recreate scenes he's seen long ago. In order to get the exact color he remembers, he often uses layers of color.

I had been thinking about priorities at the time (I do that a lot). That boy's story and my somewhat illogical thought that sprang from it deeply touched me. I pulled the car over, and with tears streaming down my emotional face, I said, "Girls, I should just pray that God would make me something like that boy. I wish he would give me one amazing ability, if I had no others — the ability to praise Him!" I suppose that was too emotional, but for some reason the girls were not shocked or upset. God was real and our love for him real when we, sitting together in a car on a warm Saturday afternoon, desired to adore Him and never let Luke 13:34 apply to us: "O Jerusalem, Jerusalem, you who kill the prophets and stone those sent to you, how often I have longed to gather your children together, as a hen gathers her chicks under her wings, but you were not willing!" This was not the last time we would talk about such things in the car.

If running around town was profitable family time, distance

driving really was. When I took them shopping and out to eat at their favorite restaurant in Springfield, when I took one or both of them with me to speaking engagements, or when we went somewhere special, like the time Stace and I went with Mom and Loren to see *Camelot*, one of the nicest things about it was being together in the car for such a long time. "Didn't you love it, Mom," Stacey asked as I paid the toll, "when Richard Harris yelled at the end, 'Run, Boy, run!' "

A lot of times Tony was with us, and my joy was really complete — I could talk awhile and sleep some, too. We must have made four hundred thousand two-hour trips home to Muskogee with the girls. It didn't matter if we were making one of those trips or going to Silver Dollar City for the fifteenth time, or driving to Tulsa to catch a plane for our one trip to California — all the trips provided lovely times together and important communication.

Just one example was the Saturday night Tony and the girls traveled to Tulsa to pick me up at the airport. As my plane landed and taxied to Gate G, I looked out the window and saw a precious sight. The airport was nearly deserted; the only person I saw in the long line of huge plate glass windows was Leanne, who stood there cupping her eyes with her hands so she could see out. Then Stacey joined her. When I thought nothing could be any lovelier, Tony walked up behind them, and all three of them stood, cupping their hands and peering into the darkness, looking for me. I knew, as I rushed in to meet them, that that was one of the "pictures of the mind" I would always cherish.

As we were walking down the terminal, the girls taking turns carrying my briefcase for me, I mentioned how special that scene had been. Stacey grinned and said, "I knew you were going to say that, Mom. I just wasn't sure when." I couldn't believe she said that. For some reason I was just slightly disgusted that I am apparently so predictable and asked her just how she happened to know that. "I just did," was her answer. This didn't completely satisfy me, but Leanne ended the matter by saying she thought it was nice that the four of us knew what each other would say in certain situations. I decided she was right. That was one of the joys of knowing another person intimately, and it came from hours and hours of being together.

That particular trip home was especially nice, at least after we got out of Wendy's where Leanne had asked for a "pita," which only Burger King makes.

When everyone got settled back into the car, I told the girls that someone had asked me at the retreat if the girls minded when I was gone speaking. I said that I had told the women that I wasn't gone often and that they didn't mind because they got to spend special time with their dad. Then my curiosity got the best of me, and I asked the girls if I had answered correctly. Leanne said no. But she was kidding. About an hour down the road, Leanne asked if she could get in the front seat with us. It was getting late and she wanted me to hold her. Usually we didn't like to crunch in the front seat of the car, but I told her I'd say yes if she said she didn't really mind when I was gone occasionally. She bargained, and the trade was made.

I was so happy to be in the car, driving to Joplin with Tony, with Leanne leaning on my shoulder and with Stacey lying in the back seat holding my hand in the air where she found it looking for hers over the seat. The soft love song, "Just You and I" playing on the radio was a nice touch. We all hummed along.

An incident that sums up all our "road" time together happened when we were on our way home from visiting friends in Hutchinson, Kansas. We had packed up and got an early start. Not as early as Tony liked, for the sun was up, but early enough that the streets were almost deserted. For some reason the girls and I were alert at that hour; thus, with a smile, the four of us each manned a window. To complete the picture, Katie — "the finest dog that ever lived" — sat on Stacey's lap and shared her window. Contentment oozed. About that time, an old car came rattling down the road in our direction. As we looked over at an unshaven, generally unkempt man, he leaned out of his car, looked at the five of us, and snarled sarcastically, "Well, if it isn't the happy family!"

We were in mini-shock as we drove off. What an odd man. What an odd thing to say to strangers. Then we laughed, because we must have looked quite revolting to that man on such a bright morning; we practically gleamed with good will. If we could find him today, several years later, we would thank him for giving us our label. What fun we've had with it. We say it all the time, like when we're driving to church: "Well, if it isn't the happy family, minus one" (Katie doesn't attend church).

Chapter Eight

"Come Share Your Lives With Me"

We always enjoyed being home together, too. Home was warm and kind and safe. It was a nice retreat for all of us, but for the girls it provided great security. One afternoon after a hectic morning at kindergarten, five-year-old Stacey caught me in the playroom and threw her arms around my leg. I felt like I was in a vise and immediately deduced that perhaps something was amiss. I knelt beside her and said, "Stacey Bug, what's the matter with my baby?" She couldn't say much; she just sighed and said, "Oh, Mama, I wish I were four again!"

What a thing for such a young child to say. But she wanted to be four so that she wouldn't have to go to that awful kindergarten each day. For many children kindergarten is a wonderful experience. My girls were mature enough that it should have been for them. I would like to think they didn't like it because home was too nice and they couldn't stand leaving for even a morning, but I really think, in this case, they didn't like it because of the teacher (that's hard for a teacher to say). Both girls started their educational career with the same teacher, a woman who might have liked children at one time, but that was probably long before the girls showed up, just before her retirement.

Leanne's dilemma will give you an idea of just how scared they were of her. One day she came home from kindergarten with the dreadful news that she had thrown up on her desk at school. I was shocked, because one of the really nice things about both girls is their ability to throw up in very convenient places. (A fact that irritates my mother ever so slightly since I thought the appropriate place for throwing up was beside my bed, if not in it.) I questioned Leanne about how such a horrible thing could have happened. Her explanation made sense. She said she raised her hand, and then before the teacher saw her, she put it back down. Then, getting sicker by the minute, she raised her hand again. And put it back down again. But it wasn't long before she knew she must say something and back up her hand went. But as before, she put it down before her should-have-retired-sooner teacher saw her. She kept putting her hand up and then down, because she did not know exactly how to phrase her request for such a frightening woman. Should she say she had to throw up, or should she use the more formal word vomit? She wrestled with this decision until there was none to make.

When Stace got home and we had our usual after-school visit, we decided Leanne actually had many more options. She could have said "Up-chuck," "toss my cookies," earp, retch, or even regurgitate. By the time Tony got home, it all seemed pretty funny.

What seems awful is made ok at home. Most days the girls

and I spent half an hour or so talking after they got home from school. I wasn't the kind of mother that prepared treats to give the kids when they got home from school, although if I had it to do over again, I might be. I would do it, however, only by God's grace, because doing such a thing would never come naturally or easily for me. Don't get me wrong, we almost always had a snack. It just wasn't special. Unless you call canned biscuits and honey special. Sometimes there were cookies and cake, but not unless they very nearly walked in off the street.

Still it was always nice to relax together after our hard day. Sometimes we all worked together in the kitchen, either scrounging up a snack or preparing an early dinner. Sometimes we'd play an Amy Grant album and have a concert in the kitchen. There was an inherent problem with that, though, because for some reason, when we all sang in the kitchen, Katie, our beloved miniature schnauzer, insisted one of us hold her and rock her back and forth in time to the music.

During their teen years, the girls and their friends laughed at me, because almost every day, I'd say, "Girls, come share your lives with me." And they did. It could be any time of day; I've already mentioned bedtime, but this time after school was great, too. I remember hearing about a young man that missed his mother so much after school that he went into her closet and pressed his face against her clothes. Although that sounds a bit eccentric, it points out how much children like to be with their mothers. Another journal entry I read reinforces that idea, too. A young man wrote how much he loved it when his mother would ask him to go on a walk with her, because during that time he had the full attention of this busy woman.

Our unplanned afternoon time was so nice that at one point I tried to structure it. We committed ourselves to forty-five minutes after school for quite awhile. Such things as telephone calls (I understand there is a device you can put on the phone to eliminate the ring) and homework waited. Between twenty and thirty minutes of this time we spent having devotions. All four of us had tried many different time frames for having formal devotions. For awhile we had them at six in the evening. That was interrupted too often, so we switched to 7:15 in the morning. That was better, but the mother has to be very sharp to make that work consistently, and I wasn't sharp enough, I'm afraid. The people I know who have daily family devotions most successfully, especially with teenagers in the home, have them in the morning at breakfast time. We gained so much from praying and reading together regularly and formally. We forfeited a lot when we didn't do it consistently.

The girls and I called this forty-five minutes after school "Our Time." It was a pleasant, happy time, and if I had been more disciplined, we might have had it always.

But even when it was unstructured, as it ended up being more often than not, we were blessed enormously. During this time we discussed the lives we were living, often laughing or crying, often stopping to pray together.

Some of these afternoons turned into teaching times. One day while we were talking, it came to my attention that Leanne had looked at someone hatefully. That may not sound too serious, but given the way we believe and what we desire for our lives, it really was. Sometimes Leanne can look at people like they are uncommonly stupid. She really would never want to hurt anyone, yet her "look" has that potential. This afternoon I decided I needed to talk to her seriously about it. Although she was probably too big for it, I put her on my lap as I confronted her. She wouldn't look at me, and as I talked softly to her, tears trickled down her face. She knew it was true, and she was sorry that it was. I knew how she felt. One of the few times I remember my dad punishing me was when he hit me over my smart-aleck head with a loafer for looking at him like he was pitifully lacking in good sense. I hated criticizing her; on the other hand, I wanted to teach the girls responsibility in all areas of their lives, including calling "a spade a spade" as they look at themselves. I have seen kids, and adults, too, who cannot do that. Nothing is ever their fault. Self-awareness and the growth such awareness can bring is something they never achieve.

That was about as close to a lecture as we usually got. All the things I could have told them in a lecture were passed on around the table or in the family room with Stacey stretched out on the couch and Leanne Leech resting with me on the recliner.

In moments like those, I was so glad I was able to have a job that enabled me to be home when the girls were. For three years I had taught high school in a little town close to Joplin and hated that I could not get home before the girls. Also in moments like those, I wished that I had put off going back to college until the girls were in school all day instead of being gone for half the day starting when they were three and four. I had some pretty good reasons for going, and some of their part-time care-givers enhanced their lives, but I still wish we had had that time.

The girls are excellent care-givers at the day-care at which they work, but they have both decided after working there that they will try very hard not to leave their pre-school children in a day-care, especially full time. So many things are an ordeal for some children: like merely getting a snack; like endless lines, simply to go to the bathroom or out to play. They hope life can be simpler for their little ones. The girls love the children they care for, but they feel like they can never hold enough, read enough, listen enough or laugh enough for all the pre-school children who need all those things.

They are sorry for the families that seem to have no option. Many mothers and fathers do find ways to help compensate, though. They do some neat things to "communicate" love and warmth, even when they have to be away from their children. One mother hides a surprise for her son every day. He might find it in his pocket, his lunch box, or in his glove. But somewhere every day he finds a note or a treat that reminds him his mom cares. I also know of mothers who have worked it out with their employers to have their afternoon coffee break at the time their children come home from school. Those mothers and their children spend that break time on the phone, catching up on one another, finding one more way to say "I love you."

The girls and I were lucky. I don't think we took those moments at home for granted either. We knew they were significant, that they were what memories are made of. If I shall always remember "all their beautiful noises," I truly believe they shall always remember their mom saying, "Girls, come share your lives with me."

Chapter Nine

"We Don't Want to Be Teenagers"

One day when they had not been in junior high very long, we sat at the kitchen table having our usual talk. Actually, things weren't quite usual. First, the girls had fixed the snack and had it ready when I got home. They had set three places at the table. We feasted on cake, chips and Dr. Pepper. (I don't know why we're all still relatively healthy today.) Second, I noticed that even though they had had fun setting up my surprise, they seemed somewhat down. I don't know which one of them answered when I asked what was wrong, but I surely know what she said: "We don't want to be teenagers."

That was a significant statement, especially considering what happy teenagers they turned out to be. When I asked them why they didn't want to be such a glorious thing, they told me it was because they didn't want to dislike their dad and me. When I laughed, I think they realized maybe that would not have to happen. But they had been observing. They were on the bus with teenagers now, and it seemed all of them had bad things to say about their parents and about home. They thought maybe that was a requisite for teens, and they really dreaded it.

There are probably a lot of reasons their teenage years were some of the happiest ones we had. A couple of them have nothing to do with Tony and me. Our girls were not strong willed, and since they had each other, they had built-in positive peer pressure. Negative peer pressure, I'm sure, has marred a lot of homes. So although we had the ordinary problems to deal with, we did not have extenuating circumstances. They say God will never allow you more than you can handle, and the girls may be proof He didn't think I could handle much.

On the other hand, some of the reasons the years were happy probably did have to do with us. It may have had to do with what we demanded of them and what we demanded of ourselves.

If our home were to provide safety and warmth, if it were to be a retreat, a haven, all of us had to contribute. One thing we did not allow was for the girls to talk disrespectfully to us. Rudeness and disrespectfulness goes beyond the noise pollution I will tolerate. We just would not have it. In time, they noticed when their friends or acquaintances talked rudely to their parents, and they told us how glad they were that they were never allowed to talk that way.

It's not that it never happened. Every so often, they were on the brink of it. I remember one time when we were in Muskogee where both my family and Tony's live, I took the girls shopping. While the three of us were in the dressing room, Stacey said something that I considered both rude and disrespectful, and instinctively, I smacked her mouth. I'm not advocating that, but I'm not advocating letting it pass either. Unfortunately for me, if you rub a feather over Stacey's skin, it leaves a mark. If she scratches her arm when it itches, it leaves red welts. More unfortunately, it was time to return to the Stark clan. Everyone saw that Stacey's mouth was a bit red and wanted to know why. So I told them. And if I remember right, I told them without apology, saying we did not allow that sort of talk in our family. Violence, yes. Impertinence, no. (Just kidding.) No one seemed to be totally satisfied with my answer, and Stacey could not stand it. She told them that she did not want to be allowed to talk to anyone the way she had. She went on to say that she was glad I had disciplined her. She finished by saying I had barely touched her. I found it interesting to hear her defend her brute of a mom.

Something else we asked of the girls was their participation in our "society." I mentioned earlier that we tried to teach them responsibility in every area of their lives, and we thought it very important for them to help around the house. Actually Stacey was the first one to bring it up. When she was in the fifth or sixth grade, she asked for an allowance. I decided that was a pretty good idea but informed the girls that weekly responsibilities, called chores, went along with a weekly allowance. I told them it would be great: they'd feel pride in their contribution to the family and excitement at having their own money to spend however they wished. They were pleased; I think they thanked me.

Later I made a list of chores and gave it to them. Stacey stood before me, amazed at what she considered a lengthy list. She looked at the list and then at me, several times. Finally, she said, "What exactly is it, Mother, that you'll be doing?" A rare slip in her usually grateful spirit. Oh well, she recovered. The girls have run the vacuum sweeper so long now that when they leave this summer, they will have to tell me where it is and how to operate it. One time I came around the corner of the family room just in time to see Stacey plug in her old friend the sweeper, grab its handle and say to it: "I'm Big Tex, and I mean to tame you." Something like that hardly deserves the label "chore."

Tony and I really did think they needed to get used to contributing. A by-product of this was that because we all pitched in and worked together, then we could all enjoy playing together or we could all enjoy some time to do our own thing. Because of this, they were spared the martyr-mother routine, a routine we sometimes bring on ourselves by not demanding what is only civil. Another by-product was that they know how to do their part. Tony and I have watched them become valued workers and dependable members of any group they are part of. Working together was as beneficial for us as playing and praying together.

The second principle that seemed to make our home reasonably warm and kind was that Tony and I knew how to apologize. We just didn't have perfection down and have never pretended to. In fact, I had to apologize to Stacey for my part in the dressing room fiasco. I had provoked her, even though I know the scripture well about not provoking our children to anger.

It wasn't the first time I had had to apologize. One of the first times, she was barely two. Unlike a lot of people, I believe in limited spanking of young children. At some point, though, children become old enough that that particular punishment does not teach or restrain, but only embitters. In this instance, even though Stacey was young enough still to be spanked, I should not have spanked her, because I did it out of frustration. I had worked hard all day and even waxed the hardwood floors in her bedroom. So when she stood there, pretty much potty-trained, and wet all over that floor, I reacted. I picked her up too swiftly, spanked her legs and whisked her into the bathtub. I still can't believe I could have been so mean. I don't remember ever communicating to her before this that I had done something wrong. But as I tucked her into bed a little later, I told her that although I felt she should not have stood there and wet all over the floor, I surely should not have spanked her for it. After all, I was twenty-three making a mistake; she was only two. I told her I was really sorry. I did not make a practice of apologizing for discipline, but this apology was for unacceptable motive and unreasonable behavior. She looked me right in my eyes and inserted the knife with gentle innocence. Putting her little hands on both sides of my face as I sat beside her and bent over her, she patted me and said, "That's ok, me mama, you do it for me own good."

I'm sorry to say, it's been eighteen years and that has not been wiped out of my memory. *She* forgot, though. Children are kind. She even forgot one of the meanest things I did when she was in high school. We were trying to encourage her to get back into the habit of doing her chores again without being told and when they were supposed to be done. (I know that gets to be boring — ask me.) So one day I came home after they had been there awhile. I was dead tired, and as I put my things away, Stacey told me she had run the sweeper. "But have you dusted?" I snapped, "That's what I care about." She turned around and walked away.

Without hitting me, surprisingly enough. Can you imagine? Even as she walked up the stairs, I was dying. How could I have said such a thing? I didn't even mean it! Please, God, tell me it's PMS; tell me my hormones are going wild and this isn't the way I really am. I found her and asked her to forgive me. I told her that she is the best vacuum sweeperer in the whole world (which she is), and I told her all the other things I had felt downstairs. She forgave me, and unfathomable to me, she forgot.

Sometimes our children think we are upset with them when we aren't at all. So not only did I apologize when I needed to, I also explained to them when they were very young that most of the time when I get upset and slam a cabinet, it has nothing to do with them. That comforted them; somehow it made them feel more secure to understand that.

As awful as all these revelations are, I really would have to say that we tried hard to be loving and respectful to one another, and we almost always were. But if we were unable to live perfectly, at least we knew how to be sorry and how to forgive. One other thing — we tried not to take advantage of one another. We tried hard to live so that we didn't have to be sorry too often.

Home should be the safest place in the world. That's probably much of the reason we are so horrified to read or to see on television accounts of child abuse. Our minds can hardly accept what happens to great numbers of our children.

In our living room hangs a stenciled picture of little houses inside a large heart. Underneath the heart, it says "Love is nice to come home to." I am so glad that when we came through our door, we were "safe."

Chapter Ten

"But Will You Still Love Me?"

Something didn't feel right when we woke up. Where was the obtrusive alarm or voice announcing a day I was never quite ready to start? No, the sun shone too brightly behind the blinds, and I was entirely too rested and ready to get up. Before we could look at the clock to see that it was well past seven and that Tony and the girls were late, Leanne came stomping into our bedroom with a huff. She was articulating faster than I thought possible. Her thesis was that Tony and I had some nerve letting her sleep this late, making her late to school. The verbiage didn't die out as I would have expected. It went on and on as she made her way to the shower in our bathroom. Finally I stopped it. "Enough, Leanne. That is noise pollution, and I don't want to hear another word. This is the situation, and now the four of us will deal with it the best way we can. And without any more of your comments. Furthermore, set your own alarm!''

With that she stepped into the shower, and I went downstairs to fix breakfast. Leanne's uncharacteristic outburst had astounded me. I turned on the electric skillet to heat, got out eggs, bread, milk and Crisco oil. If they had to start their day out late, I would at least make them one of their favorite breakfasts: french toast.

Have you ever been so upset you did everything in triple time? That must have been Leanne. I still had the unopened package of Bunny Bread in my hands when I saw her walk into the family room and plop down on the gold love seat. She looked pretty nice. No one in her high school would guess it had taken her seven minutes to get ready.

Taking a minute I didn't have, I walked over to Leanne, bread in hand, to add a few more points to what I had said earlier. I really wanted her to know that had been no way to begin a day. "Do you understand what I mean, Leanne?" I asked in conclusion as I moved toward the kitchen. I heard nothing in reply.

Let me get this straight, I said to myself. First she screams at us when we're hardly awake; second, she sits through a perfectly lovely explanation of earlier events with her arms crossed and her eyes straight ahead; and third, she does not answer when I ask a question. Inappropriate behavior!

Before I could think, I acted. I raised that Bunny Bread high into the air and brought it down right on top of Leanne's shimmering tresses. The sack split in half, and the bread cascaded over her like a waterfall in slow motion. I stared in disbelief. Little had changed: Leanne sat with her legs crossed, the one on top swinging fairly fast; her arms were still folded across her chest; her eyes still stared straight ahead. Only now, she sat with twenty or thirty bread slices all over her, from the top of her head to her shoulders, to a few plastered on her chest, and on down to her lap where several finally landed. I hardly knew what to say. So while I figured it out, I walked into the kitchen to get another package of bread so that I could get the toast on.

Unfortunately, there was no more bread. Oh, that was the worst. With only seconds to think, I went back to the gold love seat and started picking up the only bread we had in the house. I could hardly suppress a giggle when I had to ask Leanne to hand me the piece on her left shoulder and then took the last slice off her head, but I knew I had better suppress it.

The four of us ate our yummy toast in strained silence. Tony thought it stemmed from what had happened upstairs. My clearing that misinformation up was the first anyone spoke. "Tony," I said, "did you know that just minutes ago I got the bread for the toast you're eating off of Leanne's shoulder?"

Finally eyes met, and if we didn't fall out of our chairs laughing, we did smile, prelude to laughter that would come. That's the Bunny Bread story, and for some sick reason, one of our favorites.

When we started talking, Leanne said she answered me — just in a very low voice. I said that in that case I was sorry, but she must learn to speak up.

I wouldn't call that very good discipline, although it probably beats spanking two-year-old Stacey for wetting her newly polished floor. Still, Leanne was not bitter about it, probably because she knew she deserved what she got.

We had two basic rules for discipline. One, we picked our battles carefully. We knew there would be times when we would have to disagree with the girls, times we would have to say no, but we tried to say no or disagree only when we had to. As a result, I'm sure they went to school in outfits I never would have wanted them to wear, but if they weren't immodest, and they were not, I let them wear them. Peace was worth a lot. But not everything. Some things were worth the discomfort of "battle."

For instance, we thought it was worth all we went through to teach them that deceit was wrong. We thought there might be life-long consequences if we ignored what happened one Friday night. So we didn't, and we hope there will be life-long benefits.

I had been gone for the weekend and knew something was wrong when the three of them picked me up at the Joplin airport. I was talking away as usual, but eventually I realized that I was the only one talking. Then I realized the girls could hardly look at me, and Tony seemed more serious than usual. Something was wrong, so wrong that we didn't even talk about it in the car on the way home. When we walked in, Tony sent the girls upstairs and brought me into the kitchen to explain.

Tony and the girls had planned on driving to Muskogee early Saturday morning to see our folks while I was gone that day. So both of us had told the girls they could not spend Friday night with their good friend "Susan." After I had left, however, Susan wrote the most imploring note to Tony asking if the girls could please stay and she would have them home by seven the next morning. Not being very rigid, being, in fact, pretty accommodating, Tony had said ok. Everyone was happy.

It wasn't until the plans were all made and the girls met Susan at the football game that they realized Susan's parents were gone for the weekend. At this point, they should have made the decision to come home, because they knew we would never want our tenth and eleventh grade daughters to spend the night without adult supervision. But they decided to go.

I'm glad things got somewhat complicated. Some of their friends and acquaintances found out they were there unchaperoned and came out uninvited to "party." They would not leave until Susan, crying and scared, threatened to call the police.

The girls came home the next day feeling very guilty and told Tony what they had done. They dreaded telling me as much as they dreaded telling their father, and now they sat on their beds upstairs waiting for Tony to tell me and for us to come to some sort of a decision.

Although we were going to punish them, possibly even

because of it, they didn't doubt our love for a moment. Nor did they mind the discipline we administered, even when the other girls involved, except Susan, received none. They knew we were disciplining them, no matter the pain and inconvenience, because we cared.

The girls' friends could not wait until Monday to see what kind of sentence they received. They couldn't believe they had actually been grounded for a month. But even while they were laughing good-naturedly at the girls and calling them "party animals," they seemed to respect what had happened. I think the girls were somewhat proud.

Susan, too, was grounded. She and I were very good friends, and she sent me a note asking my forgiveness for her part in the deceit. My answer to her contains much of our philosophy:

Thank you for your note of apology. Leanne said you've cried a lot. The girls are sometimes amazed at my prayers, and they might be surprised that I have thanked God for their tears. Tears are such a good thing. They show you care, and they, somehow, begin to ease the pain.

And I'm so glad you felt pain when you faced the fact that you had deceived and done something we wouldn't want. I'm glad you were sad, just so sad. You didn't avoid responsibility, you didn't try to minimize what you did, and you didn't detail other people's worse sins. We are so proud of that.

I hope you can be glad for the punishment. Your tears have shown you care. In the same way, our steadfast punishment, one we felt just, one we felt might teach (for we're not quite through with you yet), shows we care. Of course, there are many ways to show it, but this is one. For our personal well-being, and for society's as a whole, we must have "laws." For many of us, our laws or rules for living are found in the Bible — we believe God has told us how to live full, complete, joyful lives. And we believe when the laws are broken, we, personally and as a people, are hurt. Always there is some price for wrongdoing. So one reason I punish is to demonstrate that — on a small scale — or to some extent. So many kids never realize that there's a price to pay for breaking whatever code they live by — the results of the ignorance are debilitating — devasting sometimes. Somehow, I think you girls will grow up knowing this. I believe when we let you go finally, we will know you are mature, responsible, able to take care of yourselves in every way, even able to bless the world you live in. Be glad for this month. Read, meditate (really), write, sit with your parents (we've so few days left like this), and rest. You all need rest.

As for forgiveness — that's as simple as pie. It is one of the basics of the Gospel I believe in and teach. It is what makes this world tolerable. It is the reflection of God Himself. Forgiveness is yours, immediate and complete — simply for the asking (Luke 15).

And with the forgiveness is a forgetting, too.

I went on to tell Susan about what happened with the girls the night I went upstairs to tell them what we had decided. As I sat down beside Leanne on Stacey's bed, Stacey stood before me with her hands behind her back. She was not crying, but she was very solemn as she told me that she was very sorry and was ready to accept whatever punishment we thought necessary. Leanne was not so stoic. She threw her body on me, sobbing her confession. I held her until she finished. After I told them what we were going to do, I told them what I later wrote Susan, that it was forgiven and would be forgotten. Leanne was crying again:

"But will you still love me?" she needed to know. For she felt she had disappointed us.

"I adore you, Leanne."

"But," she cried, "will you still like me?"

I couldn't believe such pain. "Of course, I'll still like you."

"But," she had one more fear, "will you ever trust me again?"

"Yes, I will trust you."

We tried to avoid conflict, but when they needed discipline, we administered it. Our second principle was to administer discipline lovingly. I came home from work the day after our talk and put a poster on each girl's bedroom door. They left them there for several years. Stacey's poster showed cranky Garfield sitting at his desk writing. The caption underneath said, "I'm so happy here I could just barf." Leanne's poster had two snotty-looking Persian cats sitting beside each other. Her caption read, "We are not amused." They loved the posters, and the truth is, we had one of our nicest months that October.

Not only did we try to discipline in love, but we tried to be fair. The girls each had a date to homecoming the 30th of that month, which we allowed them to keep. Our purpose was accomplished without grounding them for homecoming. Their punishment seemed appropriate. After all, they had not burned down Susan's house. I've seen punishment that is so harsh and insensitive to the particular needs of a child that the brokenness and bitterness that resulted was as bad as the emptiness and fear that comes from no punishment at all.

The girls appreciated any appropriate discipline we gave them. Now, grown girls that they are, our time to teach through discipline is over. I did hear Tony mention to Stacey the other day that if she didn't save enough money for her car insurance, she can just plan on parking her car. Life is full of choices and the consequences of those choices. I think they may have learned that the easy way.

Part Two

**Teaching our children
what we know
about God**

Chapter Eleven

"He Loves You More"

My girls were surprised to know that when I was young, the chances of my having self-esteem were slim. I was too shy, too skinny and somewhat awkward. I did have a chance to turn my life around in the sixth grade when I was selected to lead the entire student body of Irving Grade School in our National Anthem. But I blew it. My turning point would have to be another day. As I stood before the crowd of students, teachers and visiting parents, including my mom who had taken off work, I felt pretty good. I could direct the song with my arm and everything. But my budding pride turned to horror when, after the first line of this most important song, I forgot the words. I felt extremely stupid, and I do not know how I stood on that stage, humming and smiling through the last bitter note. I was probably in shock. As I said, my turning point would have to wait. This incident was not an esteem builder.

Unfortunately, I can remember a worse one. This is the only time in my life I recall deliberately being cruel to another human being, and as fate (or God) would have it, Mother witnessed it. When I was about thirteen, a family leased the house next door while our neighbors were away for a year. The family included a fifteen or sixteen-year-old retarded boy named "Bailey." One evening all the neighborhood kids were on our porch playing and talking, until eventually we began "discussing" Bailey.

At this point I decided to be cute. With all the kids watching, I pranced across the yard, knocked on the door, and with one hand on my hip, a twinkle in my eye, and my most bewitching thirteen-year-old voice, asked Bailey if he'd like to come out and play. In mid-mock invitation, I looked over to make sure all the kids were still watching and met my Mother's eyes instead. Such fear I've seldom known, and it was justified. That evening the rod was not spared.

I seemed to have been a sometimes unlovely child, but I knew three things that are basic to self-esteem. First, I knew that I was very important to my mother and father. Second, I knew that, despite my inadequacies and sins, they loved and accepted me. Third, I knew they wanted me to succeed, for they always encouraged me. So with all my problems, I *liked* me. They say parents can do that for their children. Many do. I'm sure we're all supposed to.

Children who have or who have had a good relationship with their parents have an easier time understanding God and His passionate love and concern for them. It is no accident that the scriptures are full of father/child figures of speech and terminology. What brings more comfort than Jesus taking time to hold the children while speaking to the masses. Or Jesus teaching us to pray by addressing God as Father. Or Jesus teaching us how God feels about us by telling the most wonderful of all stories, The Prodigal Son. No sweeter image exists than the father, seeing his son while he was still afar off, running down the road to embrace him, kiss him and celebrate his return. This is the only time God is personified as running.

We wanted the girls to know that the creator and sustainer of the universe was their loving father. We wanted them to know God and did our best to teach them everything we knew about Him. We wanted them, in a world in which most people are oblivious to their spirit selves, to "seek first the kingdom of heaven."

The girls knew how Tony and I felt about them and how "good" our lives were because of them. We taught them that God desired such a relationship with them. We showed them that God's word makes it clear how important we are to Him. We wanted them to take these passages very personally, as we did. For instance, God calls us his inheritance (Eph. 1:18) and calls himself rich because of it. What a thing — for him to call us his inheritance. Why are we, as God's inheritance, so valuable?

I would say that for the same reason any inheritance is valuable. For some people an inheritance may only mean monetary gain, but for many of us, it is much more than that. The girls have already decided who will get my apple ring and the antique blanket chests. They come by that honestly. My mother and father may leave me some money. but that is not the inheritance I will cherish most. I will cherish what they give or have given me that has been part of them — my mom's wedding ring, our old pictures, three generations of letters, an old china closet, their Bibles and the other books of study they have pored over since they gave themselves to God, the glasses they have worn that remind me of them, a key ring I gave Daddy that he told me he loved.

These are love, and these are my inheritance.

An inheritance is not anything one can purchase. That's part of why it is so valuable. No amount of money could buy

Daddy's key chain or Mom's ring if they were given to someone else. And that, I suppose, is part of why we, as God's inheritance, are so important. We are a love gift, and the one gift that God cannot give himself. The girls feel good knowing they are so significant.

They also learned he loves and accepts them as they grow to the spiritual maturity of the two great commandments — loving God and man (Matt. 22:37-40). I must have been in my late twenties before I finally understood and truly believed that. I have messed up a lot. I used to dislike myself when I sinned. I wanted just to give up. What I needed to understand is that, like my parents, God is a patient, forgiving teacher. Until we understand that, we blame ourselves, dislike ourselves, dwell in our inadequacies and cannot even begin the long, laborious, but glorious process of knowing and loving God and man.

The Word so clearly tells us that God is merciful, that He has compassion on his children, remembering that we are dust (Psa. 103:12-14). He shows us His mercy, too, in the stories about the lost coin, lost sheep, and lost boy (Luke 15). I had to learn what seems obvious, but isn't — that even God's most faithful and beloved servants experienced fear, failure and sin.

Abraham and Jacob lied and deceived.

Moses offered excuses, afraid to do what God asked.

Samson forgot the source of his strength and behaved unbelievably foolishly.

David committed adultery and murder.

Jonah was rebellious, stubbornly going his own way.

Martha was concerned about relatively trivial things instead of being in the presence of Jesus.

Peter swore his love and allegiance to Jesus and with practically his next breath, denied his Master.

But life for them was overcoming, or should I say, becoming. And as I "became," I finally learned that I will not be perfect, but that I am reconciled and redeemed, washed white as snow, blameless because of Jesus. Meanwhile, our Father is working in us; it is a continual process: "He who began a good work in you will carry it on to completion until the day of Christ Jesus" (Phil. 1:6).

As I deal with my failures and sins and overcome them, I feel God's pleasure, to borrow a phrase from *Chariots of Fire*. One of the problems I've struggled with as an adult is a temper. I've embarrassed myself more than once. I used even to get mad because I got mad. I really had some growing to do in that area. I believe that I began overcoming when I came to understand two things: (1) God did not think I was an awful person because sometimes I failed to control my temper: (2) He *did* want me to be victorious over it and was happy with the victory.

About that time, Leanne was learning to ride her bike, and I began to compare my overcoming to her endeavor. Leanne was only three when she decided to master bike riding. Stacey was four and had made a conscious decision not to learn yet; she reasoned one could be hurt doing such a thing. So Stacey, with her hands behind her back and her head shaking back and forth in wonder, stood beside Tony and me as we watched Leanne climb on her two-wheeler. She was so young, so little; she didn't even have the hang of braking. To stop, she used to run into the garage and crash. Leanne mangled a lot of bushes, flowers, skin, as well as the garage door before she learned to ride well. How did Tony and I respond to such ineptness? We never once yelled at her, put down her efforts, or ridiculed her failures. That would have been unthinkable. Instead, we encouraged her, took pleasure in her successes — fixed the garage door. I began to picture God and me that way as I struggled to overcome my anger or anything else. It was a good, positive feeling, so much better than the negative that kills the spirit utterly.

The happiness of my new perspective changed my life. The girls have heard me tell about it often. I'm glad to say that I seldom get made at people. For some reason I get mad at in-animate objects. As I said, I have been so embarrassed by my unreasonable behavior. I was very hateful to our green

Lawnboy lawnmower when it wouldn't start. I stood out in the hot sun and pulled that cord for a solid hour. All in the world I wanted to do was surprise Tony. Instead I surprised my neighbors when I verbally abused the deceptively innocent-looking mower. I finally gave up on the thing. As I walked up the three steps into the house, I looked down on it and told it through clenched teeth that I hated its guts. Not good. But verbal abuse is somewhat preferable to the physical. I'm horrified to say that I physically abused a $10 "pre-owned" vacuum sweeper whose ancient nozzle kept falling off. After I had bent over and put that nozzle back on fifteen times, I snapped and beat that nozzleless wand all over the living room rug until it was pretty much bent beyond repair. Tony made me "run the sweeper" with a broom for several weeks after that. I have endless examples; Tony was shocked to realize the woman he wed would yell at a mascara tube for falling from her hand and landing on her foot.

The good news is that I'm improving.

After I had been working on this problem for a very long time, and after I began to understand God is an encouraging father instead of some sort of disappointed, impatient judge, something wonderful happened. While making a peanut butter and jelly sandwich one day, I dropped a brand new economy-size jar of Welch's grape jelly all over the just-mopped kitchen floor. Now, there was a time that would have upset me greatly. This time, however, I just looked at it. I was not in the least bit mad. I'll never forget that before bending down to clean up that sizeable mess, I looked out my kitchen window at a place where I thought God might be at that moment and said, "You probably think that made me angry!" And then I smiled. And I honestly thought God smiled back. The victory was being won.

Victories are still being won, because I have finally understood how loved I am and that I am sanctified and justified (I Cor. 6:11), the adopted, bought-and-paid-for, precious, beloved child of the king. So I have learned to be happy with myself when I win victories, tolerant with myself when I lose, and when I lose, I tenaciously try again. That attitude protects self-esteem. It makes our lives what God intended them to be.

Naturally, I had to tell the girls. I am so glad that they have accepted their God and realize what it means to be his child.

It is profoundly sad when people choose not to. I've tried to imagine how God felt when man separated himself from God. I think I caught a glimpse of it several years ago, sitting around a smokey table in a tiny, utilitarian, cement-block room. The professor lectured his graduate students over Book XII of Milton's *Paradise Lost* and then read the closing lines, where Adam and Eve, banished from Eden, look back on the eastern side of Paradise:

> Some natural tears they dropped,
>   but wiped them soon;
> The world was all before them,
>   where to choose
> Their place of rest, and Providence
>   their guide:
> They hand in hand with wandering
>   steps and slow,
> Through Eden took their solitary way.

I may have been the only student who knew the lines we were hearing were more than beautiful poetry. I know I was the only one brushing tears away. Tears seemed strange in that room. But I couldn't help it. I couldn't help wondering how God must have felt watching his creation as they walked away from Eden.

I do know what he did, though, He kept on loving us and wanting us. And after ages of careful preparation (Heb. 1), He sent us His own Son as a sacrifice to restore us to Him. Now, in our lives, Eden can be reclaimed.

Man responds in many different ways. Some believe in no God. Some believe in the creator God but are hostile to Him.

Some choose to worship other "gods" or God's creation or Satan or even themselves. But more are just apathetic and unaware, like the people in the last line of Elizabeth Barrett Browning's poem:

> Earth's crammed with heaven
> And every common bush afire with God.
> But only he who sees takes off his shoes—
> The rest sit round it and pluck blackberries.

Because of these responses, the purpose of creation continues to go unfulfilled.

Except in the lives of those of us who truly love God. The Christian is the happy ending to the creation story. We taught the girls that God *is* and that He loves them. And they now refuse to be part of the masses who "pluck blackberries." They desire to "see." They have taken off their shoes. They are aware of God, overwhelmed by His creation and by all that He is. They rejoice in their reunion with God and His offer for sonship. I have observed that they are whole and happy; they are quick to say that they are. I do believe they have understood, even at such a young age, the implications of "God created man in his own image."

Both of them on separate occasions during their last year or two in high school called me into their room to tell me something. They wanted me to know that they would pass on what they knew — they would teach *their* children who God is and how much He loves them.

Chapter Twelve

"He Has Heard Me"

Paul says that "since the creation of the world God's invisible qualities — his eternal power and divine nature — have been clearly seen, being understood from what has been made" (Rom. 1:20 NIV). Always for me nature has affirmed God. Jesus' resurrection affirmed Him, too. It always seemed easier to prove the resurrection than to refute it. This was enough for me to believe; I needed nothing else.

But nothing has thrilled me more and nothing has caused my faith to grow more than the fact that I have approached God, and He has heard me (I John 5:14).

When we pray fervently, that is, dead seriously, and specifically, we will be answered specifically. Often the immature, the inexperienced, and the unbelieving are tempted to think such answers are "coincidence." But as someone once put it — it's interesting how many coincidences happen to those who pray, and how few happen to those who don't.

One of my first and dramatic examples of prayer answered and God's presence felt was when I prayed a prayer that didn't seem at all "good enough" to bring before the Creator of all that is. But He honored it.

I was only twenty-three when Stacey was less than two and had that life-or-death operation I mentioned. Before they could do the procedure, however, there were the preliminaries to be taken care of. A nurse came into the room and asked me if Stacey were potty-trained. "No," I gasped, thinking, of course not, she's not even two! The nurse explained to me that if she were not, then they would have to catheterize her in order to get a urine sample and to prepare her for surgery. I couldn't stand that. I knew what catheterization was, and my mind could not conceive of such a tiny child having to have that done. So with little hope on anyone's part, I asked them to bring me a potty chair and to leave my baby and me alone for just a little while. I felt like a baby myself as I knelt on that cold tile floor and unfastened Stacey's diaper. As I sat beside her and held her on that unfamiliar contraption, I prayed, as always, "according to His will" (I John 5:15), "Lord, please, unless it's part of your will that I can't see or understand, please, don't let her have to be catheterized on top of everything else." Such lack of eloquence. Yet almost instantly I heard the sound that told me my prayer had been answered. My eyes widened and my mouth dropped open in traditional amazement. And, in that moment, kneeling on that hard, impersonal floor, I was aware that my baby girl and I were in the presence of God.

He made Himself known to a naive young mother that day. I remembered His name — "I Am." And I knew why Abram fell on His face before God when the Lord made himself known to him (Gen. 17:1-3).

I have had His presence confirmed again and again.

Sometimes not only do I feel His presence, but I think He must be smiling at my astonishment. (I will admit that is somewhat subjective.) The night I took my comprehensive exams for my Master's degree, I could hardly wait to get home and tell Tony and the girls what happened. Especially the girls. I would never keep something like that from them, which is just one of the reasons God is so real for them.

I had prayed about the test a lot. I suppose some there that evening passed without that kind of petitioning. But that evening, I more than passed, for I knew God was there with me in that ugly, cement-block room.

As I quickly looked over the group of questions, I was astounded to find that I could isolate from each of the three groups (Early English Period, Late English and American), one and only one question I could answer completely enough and well enough to pass. The American Lit question required every bit of the information in my notes on Franklin and Thoreau, and only that information. The Late English question required that I discuss Tennyson's *In Memoriam* as elegy and as philosophy. Not only had I been interested in the philosophy of it and studied it, but that lengthy poem was the only thing I had looked at in detail one last time the hour before I took the exams.

But the third question was the one that made me smile. A Beowulf question is almost always part of the Early English group. Everyone prepares for it, but often it cannot be answered because some comparison must be made to a work we had overlooked. I may have been the only one to answer that question that night, because we were asked to compare Beowulf to the epic hero — Abraham! I had never been taught that or even thought of Abraham in those terms, but I knew the characteristics of the epic hero, and I certainly knew the life of Abraham. I was able to write a six-page answer that was accepted. One more time I felt God smile, and I smiled back.

If I was ever not going to tell the girls about a time when I felt God's presence, it would probably be the morning I did something strange (even for me) in a personal devotion time. I had the house to myself when I sat down to read and pray in the family room. I was reading through different books of the Bible for my devotions and had decided to read Luke next. But for some reason, I was dreading the first chapters which I estimated I had read or heard at least a million times. I was so hesitant that I decided to tell God how I felt. I asked Him to bless the reading and to forgive me for dreading it so. Then I read the first two or three chapters, including the passage where Mary asks of the angel, "How will this thing be?" The angel told her the Holy Spirit would "come upon" her and that the "power of the Most High" would overshadow her. The angel also told her "the holy one to be born" would be called the Son of God. "For nothing is impossible with God" (Luke 1:35-38). Later when Mary visits her cousin Elizabeth, part of Elizabeth's greeting is, "Blessed is she who has believed that what the Lord has said to her will be accomplished" (Luke 1:45).

During my prayer that followed this almost dutiful reading, the strangest thing happened. I made the statement in my prayer that I wished God would work in me and make me proper and, even, pure. Then I sort of laughed and muttered, "Impossible." It reminded me a little of Sara's unbelieving laugh in Genesis 18.

Then two of the verses I had just read in Luke 1 flashed into my mind as a gentle rebuke or a reminder, and it was as though God himself was in the room, which, of course, He was. Yes, "With God nothing is impossible!" and "Blessed is she who believes that what the Lord has said to her will be accomplished." I was humbled. And touched.

God has answered my prayers all my life. He answers all our prayers; it's just sometimes we don't recognize His answers or wait on them. But in each of these particular cases, the answer wasn't as important as the personal communication that resulted. This exchange was not anything I ever expected, or even thought to ask for. Sometimes I have even hesitated to talk about it. But I have always told the girls because I wanted them to know such a tender thing about our Father, and I knew they would never be so crazed as to treat God like a genie or demand a demonstration like Herod. Leanne has never forgotten the girl in high school that gave up believing in God, because He didn't leave a rose on her bed to verify that her grandmother, who had just died, had gone to Heaven.

I think it is things like that which have made me not pray about certain things. I know that I had made up my mind not to pray about selling the house a couple of years ago. It is true that we had bought a lot at a wonderful price and were anxious to build our new home so that the girls could live in it before they graduated and left. On the other hand, it was no emergency. So why bother God about something so material? I would not. And I didn't for the first five or six months. At that point, I was beginning to wonder if it would ever be sold and started mentioning that fact in conversational prayer — ever so casually. That went on for the next three months. Finally after the house had been on the market for over nine months, I began to worry. In fact, one Monday night in April at two or three in the morning I was still awake; the house was on my mind.

I was still fighting formal prayer about such a trivial matter. But a scripture hit me and I gave in — the one about casting all your care upon him (I Pet. 5:7). That's how my prayer started: "Lord, you said to cast all our cares upon you, and I have to tell you that it's three in the morning, and I think this house business has become a care." I paused at this point and asked Him to forgive me if this were an unworthy prayer; then I started casting like crazy. I told God that I truly believed our house was not going to sell unless He did it. Then I said that since I was asking Him to sell the house, I'd just ask for a few other things: I wanted Him to sell it very soon, I wanted Him to send a buyer that absolutely loved the house that I had loved, and I wanted Him to send someone with cash. There — I had done it. I thanked him very much, and with my care cast off, fell asleep

91

right away.

The next day when I came home from school at three or so, a real-estate agent stood on our porch talking to an older couple. They were from Chicago and had decided to move to Joplin to retire. They loved the house, wanted it now, and could pay cash.

I wished I had had time to tell Tony and the girls about my prayer before we had all scattered that morning. They were overwhelmed as it was, but no one could know how I felt. There must have been a huge lesson in there for me, but the main joy was not the fact that the house had finally sold. He did it again. Did he ever speak more clearly? God, the "I am that I am" (Exod. 3:14), the Creator — the Almighty *is* with us.

Every time that fact becomes reality in my life, I like Abraham, at least figuratively, if not literally, fall on my face before the almighty God.

Chapter Thirteen

"He Will Never Leave You or Forsake You"

When Stacey was only seven months old, she lay in her crib, her body jerking and her eyes rolling back in her head. I stared in horror and screamed for Tony. He calmly picked her up and rushed us to the hospital. The doctor, guessing she might have epilepsy, administered the necessary tests to obtain a diagnosis. He told us it would be several days before he could tell us anything.

I knew only one thing to do. I talked to God about it — not to inform Him, for I knew that He has been there with me as I stared at her jerking body and later as we watched them attach a million wires to her head for one of the tests. I talked to Him, instead, to acknowledge Him and to place my trust in Him once again. I prayed first of all that she might not have epilepsy.

Then I prayed that, if for some reason it were His will for her to have it or to have something else, that He gives us the strength and the grace to cope.

The hymn writer has communicated our need, our plea: "In life, in death, oh, Lord, abide with me." Of course, God answered that request long before it was ever made when He said, "I will never leave thee, nor forsake thee" (Hebrews 13:5).

It turned out that absolutely nothing was wrong with Stacey; while playing in the bed, she had probably held her breath and cut off her air supply for too long. There have been countless situations God has been there to give me whatever I needed. In some cases it hasn't necessarily been what I would have wanted at the time, but He supplies whatever we need.

Of all the names Jesus is called, Emmanuel is one of my favorites: God with us. His companionship is so sweet as we live a life that is often simple, fulfilling, and good. But sometimes life is not any of these things. Instead, it is complicated, harsh, and terrifying. Then we realize He is not only our companion, the "I Am," but He is also our ever-present protector and guide.

Ever since we were banished from Eden, earth has not been permanent or perfect. None of us is untouched by its imperfection. The girls have never expected to be. Sometimes flesh and spirit are weak. Sometimes frightening and hostile natural laws govern this temporary world. Most horrible of all, Satan, cruel and deceitful, is roaming the earth "seeking whom he may devour" (I Peter 5:8), leaving in his path despair, pain, emptiness. However some want to look at it, evil devastates lives.

But we have a faithful guide, who cares deeply about us. When the disciples were caught in the middle of a storm, Jesus walked toward them on the water saying, "It is I; be not afraid" (Mark 6:50). No one else could say that and give such comfort. That statement was, and is, full of power and authority, much like the "I AM" of Mount Sinai. It is the power that controls the wind and the waves — the power that knows when we are caught in the midst of them, literally or figuratively. We have told the girls about that. So they have come to believe that God will give them exactly what they will need for any challenge, any pain, any persecution, any handicap. Sometimes that may mean He will spare them calamity; but sometimes that may mean He will give them strength to survive it. Sometimes that may mean that they will defeat the enemy; sometimes that may mean He will give them the fortitude to regroup and attack again. Sometimes that may mean they will win a victory; sometimes that may mean He will give them the insight, patience, and tolerance that often comes with defeat.

I hope they've learned that God is there, even when He answers no. Could God have loved anyone more than His humble servant Paul? Yet when Paul prayed at least three times that some "thorn in the flesh" would be removed, God answered no. But He provided for Paul, none the less, and maybe more significantly, by giving him sufficient grace and sufficient protection. Paul learned the incredible lesson that God works in our weakness. I would hate for my girls to see in that situation a "no" instead of the great blessing. God was adequate for Paul in his infirmities, and He is also there and adequate for us in ours.

The Bible is full of stories of men and women who faced incredible situations because they had real confidence in a living God. That's how the four of us want to live our lives. Paul, who had been flogged with 39 stripes on five occasions, beaten three times, stoned, shipwrecked three times, said, "I can do all things through Christ which strengtheneth me" (Phil. 4:13). And although we haven't fought a bear, lion or giant Philistine as David did, or faced the perils of Paul, we have been afraid and will be again. But hopefully we've learned to say with Paul, "I know whom I have believed" (II Tim. 1:12) and "I can do all things through Christ which strengtheneth me."

I think I've learned to say it.

In the spring of the first year I taught English at Ozark

Christian College, I was asked for the first time to give a speech. Teaching and speaking are really not the same. So I was apprehensive at best, and scared would be more accurate. Speech giving was not on my list of things I wanted to do, but, at the same time, it seemed good to talk for and about God. So with fear as my companion, I accepted invitations.

Before every speech that spring, I knelt by my bed, the antithesis of self-confidence, and cried. That was the extent of my prayer. Then I would stand up and go speak, knowing God heard my sobs and would meet my need. I went, believing experience would one day alleviate this discomfort. I just went — God-confident.

With only a couple of speeches behind me, a real test came. I was asked to speak before a large crowd at a women's day at the college. To make matters worse, several of my friends and family members came to hear my "words of wisdom."

They met me at the house, and as they gobbled down and laughed through the carryout dinner I had brought home, I sat in a trance. Until then I hadn't realized how frightened I was. All I wanted to do at 6:00, when I was to speak at 7:00, was walk upstairs, lie down, and go to sleep. I wasn't talking, and when I tried, I could hardly put two words together coherently.

One of my friends noticed, and being sweet and concerned, suggested I take half of her prescribed diet pill to wake me up, give me some energy, and get me through this speech. Managing a smile, I thanked her and told her that I didn't mean to sound disgustingly pious, but I would just trust God to give me what I needed.

Then I went upstairs, knelt by my bed — this time too numb for tears or words — took a shower, and walked out of the house at 6:40 and into the room and behind the lectern at 6:59. Still, I was unable to talk. Oh, it does seem like I had mumbled something when we drove past the mortuary, but beyond that, not a word.

I really, truly, didn't know what I was going to do. So I

looked down, and there on the lectern by a microphone was a note that said, "Attach to your collar or lapel." I looked down at my dress with its scoop neck and laughed. That had struck me as funny, and I said as much to the audience. I what? I talked! I was going to make it. With not one second to spare, God met my need. I felt strength being poured into me, and I not only got through that hour, saying what I had come to say, but I thoroughly enjoyed it.

It wasn't but a year or two later that Leanne learned her own lesson — that God would never leave her or forsake her.

As I was just about to turn out her light one night, she burst out crying. Leanne wasn't just crying either; she was sobbing. She was very nearly hysterical, and she wasn't given to hysterics. I left the light on.

I went to her bed and asked her what in the world was the matter. She couldn't talk yet, so I held her until she could stop crying, washed her face with a cold washcloth, and waited.

Finally she told me. Her best friend at school had told her she didn't want to be her friend anymore. In a fifth grade class with twenty-one girls and eight boys, there were always problems. But this was serious. The "ringleader" of the class had decided she wanted Leanne's best friend to be *her* best friend. So Leanne found herself alone — all the more so since Leanne's former best friend had instructed her not to play with any of the other girls either.

Now it was my turn to talk, and talk I did. I said every wonderful thing I knew to say. I told her how we can't make other people do what we want them to do or be what we want them to be. I discussed the difficulty but importance of turning the other cheek, and the ugliness, futility, and self-destructiveness of any sort of revenge. In short, I said everything there was to say, and Leanne understood.

As I tucked her in again, and once more reached for the light and clicked it off, I couldn't help but think what a lucky little girl Leanne was to have a sage for a mother.

Then I heard another sob, less hysterical, but more pitiful, and Leanne said, "But, Mama, I don't *want* to lose my friend!"

And standing there in the dark, remembering all the "but-I-don't-want-to's" of my life — I understood.

With my own sigh this time, I turned the light back on and walked over to her bed once more. My ten-year-old's world was as important to her as mine was to me, and she needed help. I couldn't go with her the next day, but I knew, gratefully, that our Father in Heaven could and would. This time all I would say was a prayer:

> Dear Father, many times I have knocked and knocked and knocked, and I do not mind. But if it's in your will, please answer this request now. For I cannot go with Leanne tomorrow, but I know You can and will. Please, Father, somehow give her joy and peace in what for her has become a scary and hostile environment. I have no idea how you will do that and would not presume to tell You how if I thought I did. But I do trust You to do it. And thank You, Father, for this problem, because Leanne is going to see, for the first time in her young life, the power of her God!

At three-fifteen the next afternoon, I was standing in the living room when Leanne literally burst through the front door with joy all over her little face. "This," she announced dramatically, "was the happiest day of my life!"

She told me that everything was fine. Her friend still wasn't speaking to her, but another girl named "Kelly" needed a friend that day, and Leanne and Kelly had a great time.

The girls have learned to trust God. Leanne had a Precious Moments poster up on her wall for years that represented how she felt. It depicted a little guy with wings and goggles, standing on a cloud, looking somewhat fearfully over the edge, anticipating his first flight. Underneath the picture it said, "Trust in the Lord."

It's been interesting to watch that take root in their lives. I listened as Leanne told me about her and her fiance Scott praying about the job he was applying for and subsequently got. I heard them tell each other that whether or not they got a certain house was not a problem because they had put that in God's hands.

Stacey, too, has learned not to worry much. One day after she had just started a selling job at a shop in the mall, she called me from there. This was not the best place she was to find work. Pressure was enormous, and she was worried that they were going to fire her if she didn't sell more. One day she was doing very badly and fear mounted. She said she felt as I had about the house and hated to pray about such a thing, but she just couldn't help it. She finally asked God to help her sell something. That's why she called. She said it hadn't been any time at all after she prayed that a lady walked in, pulled two or three things off the racks and without giving it much thought at all, simply purchased them from Stacey. The total came to well over a hundred dollars. Stacey may have had her first moment of sensing God smile. She hardly knew what to think, but she knew *she* hadn't done anything.

The girls have great peace in life knowing God is with them always, and I believe they have great peace about death, too.

When the girls leave the house, I like knowing God is in control. And when I leave, they tell me to buckle up and be careful. How many times have they said it, and how many times have I replied, "I will, Girls." But whether I survive or not, I know and they know, I'm in God's care. We all "crash" ultimately. We are only headed for the "incorruptible"; we are not there, yet. So the girls know that I don't want them to be too sad some day when God finally does call me home. We are not forsaken. I will not be able to go with my girls through death, and they won't be able to go with me. But it will not be a solitary or devastating thing — not for the one who goes, and not for the one who remains behind a little longer. For we know who always abides with us.

The other day I was looking over an application Stacey had to fill out in order to go on a missions trip. One question they asked was how she felt about her relationship with Jesus. Her answer made her mother very happy:

> In one word, I would say Jesus is my peace. I feel so confident that no matter what happens to me, however tragic, I will be fine. I will be more than fine, because Jesus is always with me and would never give me more that I could bear. I take great comfort in that.

The scriptures talk about a judgment day. And Jesus will still be there, standing beside those who have chosen to be written in the "book of life" (Rev. 3:5). I like to think that while He is still confessing my name before His Father, I might hear in the distance of my mind, like an echo, those other words that will have taken me through a lifetime: "I will never leave thee, nor forsake thee."

Chapter Fourteen

"He Is Love"

When I started to school, my mother started to work. And that was when Billie came into our lives. Willie May Wakefield was her full name. She babysat and did some light housekeeping for us.

She was a big woman. And she was black. And because I, most of that time, was just a kid, I don't remember that much about her, except that — she lived alone in a dark little house, no color anywhere except for her blue telephone, she was very poor, and she cared about me.

I do remember isolated incidents, too. I remember, for instance, her braiding my hair one day, only she called it platting. I pulled away repeatedly as she pulled me toward her. Finally, she got fed up with my fidgeting and said, "Get back here, Chil'.

Dis black ain't gonna rub off on you!"

I don't know why I remember that.

I also remember sitting quietly alone on a summer morning .eating my breakfast cereal. Billie stood in the kitchen doorway with her hands on her sizeable hips, shook her head back and forth, and for some reason unknown to me, muttered, "Nina, Nina (which is what she called me), everyone think Loren (my little sister, born with a sweet smile and a halo on her head) be the nice one of you kids, but you and I knows, *you* be the nice one." Loren must have surely done something out of the ordinary to rile Billie so. And I don't have to wonder why I remember that. She was the only human being ever to make such a statement, and she only did it once.

But the thing above all others that stands out most in my memory was her calling us to feed the cat and the dog. The beloved cat and dog. That dog had been our companion since before I was born. Every evening around five, not long before she left, Billie prepared dinner for Pete and Ginger and called us kids to feed them. Evening after evening she hollered, "Kids, come feed de cat and come feed de dog!" Over and over, night after night, year after year, we heard it: "Kids, come feed de cat and come feed de dog." Imagine our horror when one evening she hollered, "Kids! Come feed de cat 'cause de dog is dead!"

All three of us kids came screaming from different corners of the house. Less stable children would probably have been permanently traumatized. Billie was not being cruel. Not at all. She was just being practical. There was just no sense in feeding that dog.

One day when I was in the tenth grade, Mama gave us the news that Billie would not be working for us anymore — after all, I did say I was in the tenth grade. We had outgrown her, and another family needed her. I looked around for Billie and realized she had already left for the bus stop and would never be back. I ran wildly from the house, across the backyard, through the gate down the alley, and finally caught her. I wasn't sure what to say. I was not very articulate at fifteen. I just hugged her and held on to her for a few moments until I saw the bus coming. Then I let her go. I turned around and walked back to the house with tears in my eyes and with a strange, sad, heavy feeling in my heart.

As it turned out, I should have been sad.

That was a long time ago. Many times through the years when I went home, I'd tell my sister Loren that we ought to take our kids and go by and see Billie, especially when they got to be the ages we were when she helped take care of us. We thought several times when I was there for just a short time that we would at least send her flowers. We should let her know how fondly we thought of her. For sure, we would get by soon.

And I'm sure we would have some day. Except Mom called me long distance several years ago and told me that Billie had been run over and killed on the expressway that now runs by her shack of a house. Mom really couldn't talk about it. Which was just as well, for neither could I. When I think about it to this day, I get that feeling like when I was walking back to the house over twenty-five years ago.

For whatever the reasons — none of them adequate — I never got by to see Billie. She never knew I cared. She was never relieved of anything by my touch — not loneliness, not poverty, deprivation, or any other kind of pain she might have had. I did not meet her needs. I did not truly love her.

And in that respect I was nothing like God. When He sent His Son, He showed us what love is. The very act of sending and sacrificing Him was love, but He showed us even more about love by the life His Son lived:

> A man with leprosy came to him and begged him on his knees, "If you are willing, you can make me clean." Filled with compassion, Jeus reached out his hand and touched the man. "I am willing," he said, "Be clean."

We have spent these years telling the girls that disciples of

Jesus love and care. As important as we think it is to be in church, that has little to do with whether we are God's child or not. Jesus tells us to love one another, and love as He loved (John 13:34). His apostle John tells us that "If anyone says 'I love God,' yet hates his brother, he is a liar. . . . Whoever loves God must also love his brother" (I John 4:20-21).

We have so much to learn about love. When Jesus looked at the crowd, He saw them differently than we usually do. He looked beyond anything surface and saw that they were "harassed and helpless, like sheep without a shepherd," and He had compassion on them (Matt. 9:36).

We've told the girls that love does not mean having a gushy feeling about everyone they meet or even having to get along perfectly with everyone. That is not love as Jesus lived it. Jesus' love was simply an active concern for the welfare of another. Love is making life better for those in our sphere of influence. I never want to forget or want the girls to forget that I failed truly to love Billie.

Jesus' love was always marked by an active concern. A casual survey of the gospel accounts reveals it dramatically. He loved all people at all times. He may have been weary, busy, or grieving, but He loved. The apex of such grand love is seen on the cross. He even loved when He was dying. He loved not only His mother and His disciples and all those who cared, but He also loved the ignorant, the indifferent, the hostile, and the evil.

His loving required much suffering, especially in His last days, yet the only reference to that suffering is His subtle statement from the cross, "I thirst." I have never ceased to be affected by that: the Son of God thirsts. For love, He suffered with dignity and silence, accepting it as worth it. On that cross hung the example I want my girls to follow.

We Americans are, by nature I do believe, a pleasure-seeking people, who at the very least desire comfort. And while I desire for myself and the girls a certain amount of that, loving and caring for people almost always require a certain degree of inconvenience, risk, or pain. I think the girls are not afraid of that prospect.

We can not make a distinction between loving and serving. Loving and caring almost always require "doing." A song by David Meece called "We Are the Reason" used to come on the Christian radio station all the time. Of all the songs we've sung together in the car, this one stands out the most; we were practically the Mormon Tabernacle Choir when we sang along with it. "We are the reason that He gave His life; we are the reason that He suffered and died. To a world that was lost, He gave all He could give, to show us a reason to live." The speaker in the song finally found that the reason for living was giving.

John warns us in his letter of something that keeps us from loving in this way. Too many of us are too busy loving the "world" to love mankind (I John 2:15-17). Our cravings, our lusts, caring about what we have, what we've accomplished, what we will accomplish — these things preoccupy us, or even consume us. Hopefully the girls have learned that the mature Christian gets it straight: love mankind, not the world.

I'm rather comforted that John wrote a statement about love that seems to be a paradox: "I am not writing you a new command but an old one. . . . Yet I am writing you a new command" (I John 2:7-8). The law of love was old since it is the very foundation of the gospel, and Jesus Himself had issued it. On the other hand, it was a "new" one in the sense that Christians need to understand more and more about what love really means. As we learn more about love, it truly is an ever-new command.

An incredible and significant thing is that God's "love is made complete in us" (I John 4:12). We are one of the main ways God loves in this world. We are His vessels. "No one has ever seen God," but all can know about Him and His love through every Christian's demonstration of it. That is God's love completed. People who call themselves Christians and do not love play a part in the world not knowing God.

I hate to say it, but sometimes loving is very difficult. Oh, sometimes it is easy to believe we "love" — until we're put to the test. For instance, are we loving to another when he's criticized us? Are we concerned about where that person is coming from and how we can make him or her feel better? Or are we just ticked? Or worse. Yes, it is sometimes hard to be concerned about the well-being of another.

And because I wanted the girls to know it, I told them about "Jennifer." I didn't want them to grow up thinking loving people was simple. One night when I was tucking Stacey in, I made pretty short work of it. When I leaned over and quickly kissed her goodnight, she said, "Are you all right, Mom?"

I assured her I was and walked toward the door. Then I came back to her bed and sat down beside her. "Actually, Stacey, I'm not quite all right. Something happened at church that bothered me a lot. But I'm in there ironing and talking to God about it, and I will be all right soon."

Then I told her a little bit about a problem so petty that I couldn't believe I was struggling with it at all. That night at church a guest speaker was scheduled. He was one of my very favorites. Since I was scheduled to be in the nursery, though, it appeared that I would have to miss being inspired this night. But then I had a brainstorm. Leanne, who would rather hold a baby than breathe, could take my place in the nursery. Sure, she would miss youth meeting, but I have yet to tell you how many youth meetings, camps, church services they have attended. One million would be a conservative estimate. I did not have a problem with her missing this youth meeting at all.

She rushed to the nursery, happy out of her mind. But when she arrived, a lady informed her that she had been in the nursery during church that morning doing her regularly scheduled duty, and she should not miss any more church by being in there again that night. Nothing Leanne said made any difference. Jennifer knew what was best and insisted Leanne leave. Leanne couldn't believe it.

When she told me on the way home, neither could I. I thought all kinds of ugly things, like how often Leanne attended functions at the church all these years compared to how often her child attended. I was sure that this one night would not matter. Not to mention the fact, it *was* my decision to make. How dare someone question or usurp my authority with my own child!

So when I got home, I went to my room and put up the ironing board. When I felt like this, I needed something to iron. And it was while I was ironing that Stace told me she was ready to be tucked in.

So there I sat, telling her of my struggle. I wanted her to see that doing the right thing, feeling the right thing, was not automatic. I told her that after I turned out her light, I would go back to my room, think about God's ways and his will, talk to Him some more about my hurt and my weakness, and then I would, by His grace, put all this bad feeling away. I would forgive this lady (whom He loved greatly, by the way) because God forgave me for my foolishness. I told Stacey that's what the gospel we believe in demands of us. I've told the girls something else, too.

Maybe not in this silly instance, but in other situations when forgiveness comes very hard, we need to realize there is little sacrifice here. When forgiving is hard, sometimes we tend to think Jesus was mistaken when He said His yoke is easy and His burden is light. "No, God, this is hard. Too hard." But if we've ever felt the freedom that comes with doing what He asks, we know that forgiving someone is much easier than bitterness, resentment, unrest, or the energy-robbing, joy-robbing desire for revenge or "justice." There is an inherent reward in loving. Jesus called it the abundant life. When we Christians wonder where that abundant life is, we ought to look into our hearts and see if we find love there.

One day after school the girls and I had an opportunity to put all these beliefs into practice. They came through the door almost in tears. When they were walking down the aisle of the bus toward the door, a little girl tripped them. When the girls were walking away the same girl leaned her head out of the window and called them bitches. To their knowledge, they had done nothing to her. They were very upset, and part of them wanted to retaliate. Maybe they wouldn't trip her or call her names, but they could at least put her in her place, or "hurt" her in some way. Then we stood in the kitchen and remembered Jesus' life-changing, life-giving Sermon on the Mount. In it He asked how we are different from the pagans if we love only those who love us. He calls us to something different; we are to love our enemies (Matt. 5:43-47).

Remembering this basic to the Christian life, we went into the family room and knelt to pray. I heard them ask God to bless this girl. I heard them express how sad it must be to want to do and say such things to others. I heard them ask God to help them care for her. I couldn't believe what was happening. They were being set free.

Never did we want the girls to think they would be children of the light just because they had Perfect Sunday School Attendance pins. There is only one question to be answered in life. Do you love? Read I John 3:11-24 again, and find that it is love, real love, that "sets our hearts at rest" in the presence of God. Sometimes our hearts condemn us, but God is greater than our hearts. He knows our problems and struggles, our weaknesses, every extenuating circumstance. As He judges, He looks into our hearts to see if we love. And the scriptures are clear, if He finds love, "we can be confident before Him." It is in I John that we also learn that perfect love takes away fear.

When I see the girls love, I am so pleased. For when they love, they are so whole and happy. Leanne was very good in high school to take time for the somewhat mentally retarded who had been mainstreamed into the school. She really cared about them, and they knew it. At the end of her junior year, several of these boys asked if they could write a note in her yearbook. They all wrote sweet entries, but one boy, in particular, really touched her. He had taken her yearbook to his next class so he would have plenty of time to write. A girl Leanne knew came up to her later and told how the young man sat by her and asked her how to spell every word he wrote in Leanne's yearbook so that it would be just right. He didn't want to mess up her yearbook. Leanne will always cherish what it took him so long to write: "Leanne, you are a good person and my best friend."

The girls have found much reason for living. They have known the fulfillment that comes with loving and giving. I'm glad they've been spared the emptiness of self-seeking. Lots of people haven't been. Charles Colson in his book, *Presenting Belief in an Age of Unbelief: How to Evangelize Our Self-Centered Culture*, quotes Dorothy Sayers, an astute contemporary of C.S. Lewis. She says that the sin of our times is "the sin that believes in nothing, cares for nothing, seeks to know nothing, interferes with nothing, enjoys nothing, hates nothing, finds purpose in nothing, lives for nothing, and remains alive because there is nothing for which it will die."

Nearly all parents want their children to have certain things in life. I'm convinced the girls can do anything they determine to do, be anything they want to be. But I shall be most happy — if they can say "God lives in us and his love is made complete in us" (I John 4:12).

Chapter Fifteen

"He Is Lord"

"**P**lease go," she said. "I just can't. I wish I could. I intended to, but I can't. I really do have too much to do."

And that's the truth, I thought as I motioned for the girls to hang their coats up and put their music in the piano bench, heard the clothes tumbling in the dryer, stirred something on the stove, noticed the dishes on the kitchen counter, and remembered the two sets of papers I had to grade. Life, as it often did, had gotten crazy.

A student I had when I taught in high school was asking me to go with her to a wedding shower of a mutual friend of ours. She was one of my sweetest students; I loved the girl. "You can go. Please go. I've been drinking. I shouldn't drive. You drive,

Mrs. Stark, and take me.''

At that moment her life seemed to be falling apart. So at 6:45 I picked her up. When we got home from the shower, we sat in the car and talked a long time. She probably was in crisis. She was upset about a whole string of things, including the fact that her drinking was out-of-hand and the fact that she lived with a man that turned out to be married.

We cried together and laughed together. And as she usually did when we were together, she asked about the girls. They were in the eighth and ninth grades at the time, and she was hoping they were ok. She knew they were approaching years that could be "difficult."

I told her that as Christian parents we did worry about the girls, but I also told her that we really thought they would make good choices in the next few years. Many nights when I tucked the girls in, I would sit beside them, and brushing their hair away from their eyes, tell them to think long and hard before they, like Esau, "traded their birthright for a bowl of porridge." They must try hard not to make choices that would cause them to lie awake at night. They seemed to know what I meant. They knew people who went to bed at night and lay awake fearful, ashamed, desperate, helpless. I always wanted the girls to be able to "sleep in peace."

They tended to make good choices not only because of what they believe but also because of whom they believe in. I told my friend that night that they are not called to a church building, but to Jesus. He was worthy of their love and loyalty, since He loved us and "did not consider equality with God something to be grasped, but made himself nothing, taking the very nature of a servant, being made in human likeness. . . . And became obedient to death — even death on a cross" (Phil. 2:6-8).

I told her something else that may have surprised her. The girls knew they were not called to a set of rules: do this; do not do this. Instead, their actions, ideally, were based on what Jesus would do. What was the gentle thing, the kind thing, the good thing? Hopefully that is how they made their decisions.

I knew there would be times when they would have to be separate from some of their friends. I knew they would be "peculiar." I was glad they cared to look their best and make good grades, because that helped compensate for their incredible "strangeness." One night Stacey was standing outside McDonald's with some of her friends. One of the girls approached her and asked her if she wanted a little "something" in her coke. The girl must have been far enough gone to have forgotten Stacey never wanted anything in her coke. When Stacey said no, she looked at her and said, "How do you ever have fun?"

Those kinds of questions never seemed to bother the girls, because they knew why they did what they did. In fact, a seventeen-year-old Stacey looked back at the girl and asked her why she couldn't have fun *without* something in her coke.

Even the way they talked was a little strange. When they were very young, I discussed the ugly language they could not escape. They began hearing a steady stream of it when they boarded the school bus at eight and nine. The halls of every school should have R plastered on them for language, and even Christian schools are not exempt.

Movies lead one to believe the repetition of filthy language is the only method of adequate expression. Even though we only allowed them to attend PG ratings until they graduated, that only protected them from the dreaded F word (as well as frontal nudity and brains being blown away). Just about any other "bad" language, including God's name taken in vain, abounded.

They could have escaped it, I suppose, by sitting in their room — if they didn't turn on the radio. It is everywhere. Even on hats and bumper stickers. How could these girls keep from sounding like most of the world? How could they sound like someone who knows and loves a holy God?

I had several suggestions, but one may have been the most

helpful. I told them about the first time *I* said, "damn." It certainly was not premeditated. At the time, a "bad" word had never come out of my mouth. I was a senior in high school, walking around the stadium at a football game. Someone ran into me, and I spilled a Dr. Pepper all over myself. My response was, "Damn." I looked in wide-eyed amazement at my Christian friend, who looked back at an equally Christian me. We were horrified.

I guess I'd heard it once too often. More horror was to come. I found it was much easier to say it after the first time. I completely deteriorated in Typing II. Fortunately, I didn't progress much past the level I began on. But, unfortunately, the stopping of it was to be a life-long process. I told the girls these things and urged them *never* to let a bad word of any sort, of any degree, come out of their mouths. I encouraged them to more self-control. I urged them to be able to express themselves more intelligently, even to be quiet rather than react. I urged them to try to represent God well even in their speech. I urged them so they would have one less battle to fight, and their peers noticed their speech.

But I think their peers noticed one thing above all others. They noticed they were sexually pure. Everyone knew who was and who wasn't and exactly when it was they weren't. I think it is safe to say that fornication is the norm, even for Christian young people. In one youth group alone, I know of seven teenagers who were pregnant at one time. Even in Bible college dorms, it is not uncommon for girls to discuss their sexual experiences.

Christian young people do not seem to take God's laws seriously. But maybe they think they're one step ahead of Christian adults who don't either. They all know of ministers who have been asked to leave their churches because of an affair and of an elder who has "run off" with a Sunday School teacher.

If ungodly language bombarded the girls everywhere, so did sex. As far as the media is concerned (that is, movies, television, most books, and the radio), abstinence is undesirable, if not unheard of.

So the one thing we did not do is just tell the girls they should save sex for marriage. Instead, we tried to explore why, and we started with the fact that God told them to. We told them God created them, loved them, and wanted them to have an abundant life. That life is for those who love as He loved. But since we are slow to learn that simple yet difficult lesson, He broke love down into its parts and gave us "laws." Do not steal, do not kill, do not bear false witness, do not commit adultery. We showed the girls how all of this is subordinated under "Do Love."

The Scriptures are clear. Obeying will lead us closer to fulfilling the two great commandments of loving God and man (Matt. 22:37-39). Yet so many Christians willingly disobey.

The girls saw this graphically when at camp one year a beautiful Christian teenager asked me in a classroom setting what she could do about a sexual relationship she was having. She wrote in her note that her conscience no longer worked, and she cautioned that she could not stop the sexual activity nor could she leave her lover — both were impossible. Her willingness to break God's law and her elimination of any answer except doing whatever she pleased were typical of the society of which she is a part. She was guilty of not taking God seriously, which may be the highest form of blasphemy. She also made a wrong assumption. Stopping and leaving are difficult, but not impossible. God does not ask the impossible of us. Christians need to start living "I can do everything through him who gives me strength" (Phil. 4:13).

Christians who willfully choose sexual impurity seem to have a problem believing the Word. A minister asked a large college-age Christian group how many believed premarital sex is ok. Nearly all raised their hands. Next he asked how many believed God was a liar. Not one hand went up this time. Then he asked one final question: "How many of you believe the Bible is

God's Word, all of it?'' They all raised their hands. The minister stood incredulous before them and asked what he — what they — should do with I Corinthians 6:9-10: ''Do you not know that the wicked will not inherit the kingdom of God? Do not be deceived: . . . the sexually immoral . . . will not inherit the kingdom of God.''

We hoped that it would be enough for the girls to trust God, and as a result, obey Him. We hoped they would make Him Lord truly, and not just do His will when it was convenient. Do His will when it matched up perfectly with their own.

We also discussed all the reasons God might have asked such a thing of us, although that wasn't a prerequisite for obedience.

We talked about such consequence as developing a recreational sex mentality, which many of their friends, in fact, have developed. The promiscuous often believe they're living their lives to the maximum, in the fast lane, when actually their lives are diminished when they consider sex to be recreation only, rather than a physical union characterized by an enduring commitment. Commitment dignifies these special moments when two people come together to give one another joy and pleasure and comfort. Sex should not be less than that.

I quoted people like William Banowsky, who says that college playboys know a lot about sex biologically, yet ''despite their air of sophistication they know very little, sometimes almost nothing, about genuine sexuality. . . . In choosing to embrace sexually several persons, they are sacrificing the profound privilege of ever embracing one person as God meant it to be.''

We talked about the problems of unwanted pregnancies and venereal diseases. And we talked about the equally significant and often overlooked emotional problems. ''Free love,'' embraced by so many, has created emotional pain for the general population to the extent that it is being documented. An NBC Report, ''Second Thoughts on Being Single,'' discussed the loneliness of people who could hardly move for the crowd in the singles bars. Their loneliness had nothing to do with being alone. It had to do with no-deposit, no-return relationships. It had to do with no one really knowing and no one really caring. It probably began when they were much younger and the boys asked each other if they "got any." I told the girls I hoped they would be more than an antecedent for "any." That is the sexual experience some people have.

We also talked about the spiritual benefits of being sexually pure. God's commands are intended to shield us from pain and to help make our lives all they can and should be. In the midst of our self-interested, pleasure seeking world, some people reach beyond the physical and claim their spirit nature.

The sexually pure learn to yield to the Spirit. Holding back in any difficult area of our lives may mean that we will never turn over anything difficult. One night Stacey called me into her bedroom to read Thomas Paine's "The American Crisis, Number 1." Paine eloquently beseeches his countrymen to fight for freedom, despite the difficulty of the conflict, because "the harder the conflict, the more glorious the triumph." That applies to our Christian lives, too. " 'Tis the business of little minds to shrink," Paine says, "but he whose heart is firm, and whose conscience approves his conduct, will pursue his principles unto death." It would be good to be followers like that.

They would also learn self-discipline. Les Christie said something we liked: "People who submit to their craving for food are called gluttons and those who appease their drive for self-preservation in the face of the enemy are called cowards, but those who gratify their sexual urges are call swingers."

Sexual purity also helps to eliminate the selfishness that characterizes this world (I John 2:16) and to imitate our selfless Lord (Phil. 2:5-8). Fornicators are often self-indulgent and hedonistic. In this way fornication, adultery and abortion have at least one thing in common: "*I* wanted." God would spare us that kind of narrow existence.

The girls have taken Him up on it. Some of Leanne's friends

are constantly astonished that she and Scott have dated three and a half years and are still committed to sexual purity. They are a beautiful, loving, healthy couple who have simply made Jesus Lord. They have sacrificed little, and gained much. They have learned to love in many ways and share an intimacy that many forfeit with premarital sexual intercourse. They look forward to this summer when they will make a holy union. They shall have all the benefits we've talked about these many years. And when the years pass, I think they will have a better chance than most of staying sexually pure in marriage as they did outside of marriage, avoiding all the pain that always accompanies it. They've learned self-discipline and obedience.

The girls knew what Tony and I believed with all our hearts: we can claim to be Christian; we can go to church or Bible college, preach the gospel, teach Sunday school, be chairman of the board, or sing in the choir; we can even wear crosses around our necks or in our ears, but these things do not necessarily mean we *are* Christian. Even our verbal professions may be negated by facts. John has reminded us. He says that if we are God's people, we will love. And we will do one more thing — We will live "righteously." This becomes a possibility when we truly make Him Lord.

Chapter Sixteen

"He Is Good"

From the time the girls were very young, every time they left me to go somewhere, I'd say, "Be good." Every time I said it, they'd reply, "We will, Mama."

And that was a tall order. They knew I wasn't just talking about a system of rules that constitute proper social behavior, although they never dared to have dinner with their boyfriends' parents, lean back after dessert and burp. They also knew that I didn't mean they must obey just the Ten Commandments, although these commandments are certainly important to keep.

They knew I had something like I Peter 3:8-15 in mind. Peter tells us to be of one mind, to have sympathy with one another, to live in brotherly love, to be compassionate and hum-

119

ble, and especially, to practice forgiveness. Goodness is all wrapped up in how we treat our fellow man.

This goodness represents our Father most completely and leaves us peaceful and happy, whatever our circumstances, something the Ten Commandments are probably incapable of. We have always found this list, recorded in I Peter and several other places, to be quite a challenge. To really practice these things in all situations is difficult. Just take one thing on the list for an example. Sometimes forgiving is so hard we wonder how it can possibly be done. We know people who have struggled to forgive a husband or wife for committing adultery, or forgive a father for not loving them, or forgive a friend for humiliating them, or forgive a co-worker for costing them a job they loved. Peter can't mean to be forgiving and compassionate and sympathetic in these kinds of circumstances, can he?

The girls knew Tony and I didn't think these qualities that constitute goodness would be easy to come by. Yet we were sure that Peter, as God's spokesman, did mean for us to be these things. If he could ask it of these persecuted first century Roman Christians, who were suffering what Peter called a "fiery ordeal" (4:12), he could surely ask it of us.

I've wondered how they could be unified, humble, sympathetic, compassionate, loving, and forgiving. And then I wondered how we could be these things in our figurative, or perhaps someday literal, "fiery ordeals."

I decided four things will help. I'm sure there are other things that will, but we at least tried to do these things.

First of all we knew our attitude toward goodness must be right. We needed to love it. In his commentary on I Peter, William Barclay says there can be more than one attitude toward goodness. I'm afraid at one time or another, I've had every one he mentioned. We can be burdened by it, or we can be bored by it. Another attitude we can have, one I have too often, is we may somewhat desire it but not enough to pay any kind of price for it. However, none of these attitudes will obtain I Peter

3 kind of goodness. We must love it and desire it with our whole hearts.

We will do amazing and wonderful things when we love. I certainly cringe remembering some of the incredible, crazy things I've been able to do because I "loved." In the tenth grade I had the misfortune of adoring a sacker at the local grocery store, back when such stores were in neighborhoods, within walking distance of one's home. Now before you could understand what "love" made me do, you would have to understand how much I hate going to the store. It's almost a neurosis. I feel bad. I should be so grateful I have money to go to the store with. But, even with that kind of insight, I loathe it. I have put off going for so long that I have been reduced to running frantically through the doors to get toothpaste, Dr. Pepper and toilet paper. I'm sure I was born hating to walk those aisles. Yet when I fell for the sacker (this is pitiful to admit), I went to the store between three and six times a day. You could only go for so many things on an allowance like mine, so often I had to enlist my parents' help. They were kind. They stocked their cabinets with some pretty unnecessary items. I was so compelled that I once convinced them to fork over several dollars so that I could buy them a mop. Yes, I was even willing to do that when there were few things worse than a young teenager being seen walking down a major four-lane boulevard with a mop.

Of course, there is a very serious application of the fact that we will do incredible things when we desire something. Barclay translated v. 13 of I Peter 3 this way: "Who will hurt you, if you are an ardent lover of goodness?" Ardent lover could have been translated zealot. Zealots, fanatical patriots "pledged to liberate their native land by every possible means, were prepared to take their lives in their hands, to sacrifice ease and comfort, home and loved ones in their passionate love for their country." When we love goodness that way, we will begin to obtain it.

We also need to practice goodness. The girls joined a swim team when they were six and seven; they knew the importance of practice. You don't become a good swimmer, and you certainly don't win meets, without a good deal of practice.

In our spiritual lives, practice is significant, too. C.S. Lewis illustrates the importance of practice, or lack of it, in a passage from *Mere Christianity*:

> Every time you make a choice you are turning the central part of you, the part of you that chooses, into something a little different from what it was before. And taking your life as a whole, with all your innumerable choices, all your life long you are slowly turning this central thing either into a heavenly creature or into a hellish creature: either into a creature that is in harmony with God, and with other creatures, and with itself, or else into one that is in a state of war and hatred with God, and with its fellow-creatures, and with itself.

What a powerful thought, one to remember every time we make a choice. We should practice "good" choices in the smallest situations. Not so long ago, a lady undercharged me fifty-three cents for a liter of Dr. Pepper. I felt I had to return it, but I really dreaded it. A lot. I've learned that sometimes people think that's strange and don't even appreciate it. One time in a very nice department store, I ran into a seventy-five percent off sale. If that weren't luck enough, I found a blouse that was *my* color and my size. I seized it and rushed to the cash register where a young lady proceeded to charge me four dollars. I very kindly told her that I thought it was twelve dollars and not four. I was amazed when she backed away from the counter, looked at me incredulously, and then snipped, "Why did you say that?"

Not being very quick-witted, I muttered pitifully: "It's the creed I live by." Oh, how I hated that! There she stood. She even asked for it. This was my chance to quote Paul's Mars Hill Sermon: "I have come to preach to you the unknown God!" But no. I muttered something about a creed.

So I'm so sure that I want to take this fifty-three cents back.

Besides, I rationalized, that fifty-three cents wouldn't hurt the store. I thought they probably made that on a can of tomato paste. But the question in my mind was would the fifty-three cents hurt me — as God's child. In terms of I Peter 3, it matters a great deal. Every time we choose sympathy instead of insensitivity and selfishness, every time we choose compassion and pity instead of condemnation, every time we choose humility instead of pride, unity instead of division, love instead of the two opposites apathy or hate, and forgiveness instead of the incredibly easy malice and resentment — we are "turning the central part of us . . . into a heavenly creature."

We also need to see beyond the superficial. I remember the day I learned how little I perceive and how shallow my thinking can sometimes be. I was reading John 2 about Jesus' changing water into wine and decided to check something about the wine. As I read in Barclay's commentary on John, I realized how narrowly I had looked at this passage and what truths my elementary reading had overlooked. I was instructed that John doesn't write unnecessary or insignificant details. With this in mind, one must realize that each of the six waterpots held between 20 and 30 gallons of water, meaning Jesus provided well over one hundred gallons of wine, a quantity no wedding party could drink. What a perfect first miracle. Among many other glorious things, it shows us that "no need on earth can exhaust the grace of Christ; there is a glorious superabundance in it."

I was so embarrassed at my lack of insight, feeling I had been careless with the word or at least guilty of not looking deeply enough for all the truth there.

And in our everyday lives, we do that, too. Maybe that's a part of the reason Jesus told us not to judge (Matt. 7:1). Not only do we have our own problems to take care of, but also — we just are not equipped to judge. We seldom, probably never, know the entire facts of a situation. We often see only the results of an action — we don't know all the contributing factors that led up to it. Not only do we not know all the facts, often we misinterpret what facts we do know with shallow, hasty thinking. We must look beyond the superficial and know that life is not as simple as what we see. When we do that, we are more able to extend sympathy and love and forgiveness and compassion to a world which needs that sort of goodness.

As we strive for the "good" God desires us to be, we can do one more thing, the most important thing. We can realize that we need His help and seek it with our whole hearts. Tony, the girls, and I claim John 2 for our own. We remember the superabundance of Jesus to meet our every need. We remember that the Bible says we have not because we ask not. There is surely nothing God wants more than to help us become compassionate and loving and all the other qualities listed in I Peter 3. There are different prayers to pray at different times in our lives. The girls have learned to pray quite honestly. Sometimes we just need to pray for "spirit eyes" to *see* opportunities to demonstrate these qualities. Sometimes, unfortunately, we need to go back further and pray for a new attitude, a desire to demonstrate these qualities. Sometimes our prayer is for strength. Sometimes, courage. But the worst thing is not to ask for His help at all, which is sure failure.

God is always there for those who are willing to try. Darrel Anderson, in his short article, "His Strength, Our Weakness," tells one of our favorite stories. It is about the Polish pianist and Prime Minister, Ignae Paderewski, and a young boy. A mother took her young son to a Paderewski performance in order to encourage and motivate him. When they found seats near the front of the concert hall, the mother started talking to a friend. When eight o'clock arrived, the audience quieted, and the mother realized to her horror that her son had slipped away. To her greater horror, she looked at the lighted stage and saw her son at the "majestic Steinway," plinking out "Twinkle, Twinkle, Little Star." Not knowing what to do and before she could think of anything anyway, the "master" appeared on the stage and made his way to the keyboard:

"Don't quit — keep playing," he whispered to the boy. Leaning over, Paderewski reached down with his left hand and began filling in a bass part. Soon his right arm reached around the other side, encircling the child, to add a running obligato. Together, the old master and the young novice held the crowd mesmerized.

Anderson's analogy almost leaps off the page and has brought tears to my eyes more than once, for I have experienced this:

In our lives, unpolished though we may be, it is the Master who surrounds us and whispers in our ear time and time again, "Don't quit — keep playing." And as we do, he augments and supplements until a work of amazing beauty is created.

We need to grow to be the things Peter calls us to in I Peter 3:8-15a. Just one reason is 15b, a most familiar passage. In it Peter urges us to "always be prepared to give an answer to everyone who asks . . . the reason for the hope" we have (NIV). Maybe that charge comes here, after a discussion on goodness, because this is how it happens.

I wish so much that we could live like this, being truly "good." It would be nice if someone would look at our lives and be curious about our motivation, our source. It would be lovely to represent the Father that well.

Chapter Seventeen

"He Makes Us Strong"

One of my most treasured possessions is a sense of humor. Next to telling the girls about God and securing them a fine father, the best thing I ever did for them was teaching them how to laugh. We cry about a lot of things, but we laugh a lot, too. I'm especially glad they've learned to laugh at themselves and not take themselves too seriously. They've acquired, somewhere along the way, the ability to bounce back.

Since their father does very few stupid things, I can pretty much take credit for their understanding that one can survive terrible mistakes. I've told them what God told the "weak" to say and then lived the truth of it.

A number of my stupid mistakes have taken me by surprise. I've wakened many a morning without a clue that disaster is about to fall. Like the morning I told my high school students to "Trust me."

I'm sure every high school has at least one fire drill and one tornado drill each year. Since I was a first-year teacher, I hadn't been through the routine yet. However, anticipating a drill of some sort that day, I read the directions to my students very carefully — directions for the fire drill and directions for the tornado drill. I remember laughing (I told you we laugh a lot) at step five or six of the fire drill, which said to walk *smartly* out the designated exit. We tried to imagine exactly what smart walking looked like.

What was confusing to me, and to everyone, I suspect, was the bell. One long blast followed by a short one was the fire drill. The tornado drill was several short blasts, or the other way around; it really wasn't very clear. Late in the afternoon, the bell sounded. I was determined to do my part in this safety drill. I heard the blast and took the students to the hall. "Ok, guys, trust me. Sit down facing the wall and tuck your heads between your knees."

"Oh, Mrs. Stark!" they griped. I was in no mood; their lives were at stake. "Do it!" I shouted. I hardly noticed the other kids walking smartly by. I did notice Mr. Brotherton, another new teacher, hurry out of his room and tell his kids, "See Mrs. Stark's kids? Do that."

I got everyone settled in what I thought was probably record time when I noticed we were the only ones there. I looked down to the end of the hallway to see my principal gesturing toward the exit doors. Not being utterly stupid, I immediately shouted, "Ok, get up, you guys. We've got to get out of here. March! To the exit! Smartly!"

The kids were mortified, and rightly so. As we walked out in front of an audience of students who had been there for some time, my kids muttered, "Good grief, Mrs. Stark, you'd have burnt us up."

Maybe so, I thought, but you weren't about to blow away.

For the fourth time that traumatic first year teaching, I considered turning in my resignation. I made a lot of mistakes that year, and this one the whole school witnessed. I really did feel foolish. Not that I didn't see the humor of the situation.

I've made worse mistakes. Mistakes that weren't so funny. Mistakes that did matter. Like the time I created chaos in Sunday school, long distance.

There we were, filling the entire row. I was so happy and content to be visiting my family and attending the church I grew up in. It didn't hit me until the prayer hymn that 120 miles away, at my home church, 30 or 40 children and their teachers were waiting, the smallest ones on little wooden chairs and the older ones on squeaky folding chairs. They were waiting for me, their junior Sunday School superintendent, to begin opening exercises. I had forgotten to get someone to take my place while I was gone.

Not having a memory has caused me a great deal of grief. This had happened one other time. The senior Sunday School superintendent, and therefore, my boss, accosted me the next Sunday and said, "Jack, if you'd just let me know when you're going to be gone, I'd sure get somebody to substitute for you."

I could see it didn't make a lot of sense to him when I explained that if I could remember to call him, I could also remember to call my replacement. He tried to smile, and I assured him as best I could that it wouldn't happen again.

And it hadn't. Until that day. After we got out of the church, I told Tony I simply couldn't return to our home church. He could make our apologies the next Sunday while I began the search for a new place to worship and serve.

The man has his good points, but he can be stubborn and unreasonable, as he was in this case. He refused to leave. Consequently, the only thing to do at that point was to face the situation and deal with it and then try again to be ever responsible.

About the time I became strong again and thought mistakes like these were behind me, embarrassment gone forever, I received a blow that made me not only want to resign my job and church, but life itself.

I will tell a lot of things, but even I had to have a little space before I could tell this. The girls were there to witness that by God's grace one can survive any humiliation. They now know that one can endure anything — absolutely anything.

They had gone with me to a speaking engagement in a little Arkansas community. Tony had entered a bird dog in a field trial in the area, so he dropped us off and planned to meet us at two when our meeting was over. It was just one of those incredibly nice days. A road trip!

And it *was* nice, too — right up to the closing afternoon session. The girls and I sat on the front row while a charming young lady led us in hymns from a printed booklet, put together for this occasion. Then the song leader said she'd like to share a final song, and she started singing, "Precious Lord, Take My Hand." I looked and looked for that song in my little booklet but could find it nowhere. Oh well, that really wasn't a problem; I knew that great song of the faith pretty well. So I sang it out, loud and clear (I believe in 100% participation).

The girls, pointing frantically at Leanne's booklet, were trying to say something to me. I couldn't believe they were talking during the song service and waved them away with a look that warned they had better behave appropriately.

About the time I straightened the girls out, the song leader asked if I wanted to come up and sing the rest of the song with her. I thought this was extremely unusual; I am a pretty good singer, but this had never happened to me before. Two song leaders. How strange. As I approached the podium, I said something about how nice it would be to have all the words (I was a little rusty on the middle verses).

I was up there standing beside her about 30 seconds before I realized why she had summoned me: she had not been sharing a final congregational song — she had been trying to sing a special number. That's what the girls had been trying to show me on the program that I had pompously refused to look at.

Every time I tried to make myself feel better by telling myself this was a very small group of women whom I never had to see again, I counteracted that with a mental picture of various speakers around the country, in various meetings, bursting out in song with various soloists.

Dying was my only answer.

When Tony pulled up two hours late (I had 120 minutes to apologize over and over and over to anyone who would listen), the girls ran out and told him what I had done (they are not cruel — this was just extraordinary). Tony, for the second time in his life, laughed out loud. Guffawed.

The next day I found myself where I find myself every so often — alone on the couch, curled up in the fetal position, asking God to strike me dumb (dumber). I told Him I wasn't leaving the house anymore. Well, I didn't "tell" Him anything, but I never wanted to be vulnerable again, and I begged Him to let me life out my life on that couch.

That has been one of my recurrent prayers. I have prayed it several times when I've made a fool of myself. I've prayed it even more sincerely when I had done more than just make a mistake that embarrassed me. I've wanted to quit when I've made errors in judgment and mishandled situations with God's children. I've wanted to quit when I sinned in some other way (see chapter 11).

However, although I feel like dropping off the world when I make these kinds of mistakes or commit these kinds of sins, I know God doesn't want that.

Peter might have felt the same way at the mount of transfiguration (Matt. 17). Peter, James and John had gone with Jesus to see something very important. Jesus was again trying to help them understand who He was, using this beautiful demonstration. Jesus, His face shining like the sun and His clothes white as light, was joined by Moses and Elijah. A cloud came over them, and God said, "This is my beloved Son, in whom I am well pleased; hear ye him." Then Jesus stood alone.

One thing they were being taught was that Jesus was superior to the law and the prophets. Can you imagine how impressed the three must have been to see these representatives of both. Moses. Elijah. It must have been overwhelming. Perhaps James and John didn't realize the significance of this moment at first, but at least they kept quiet. Peter, on the other hand, broke in right in the middle of the awesome event with the suggestion that they build three tabernacles. He displayed with that statement his lack of understanding and insight. The transfiguration is also recorded in Mark 9 and Luke 9, and those accounts state that Peter really didn't know *what* to say. This would have been a good time for silence.

I've often wondered how Peter felt after he did speak. He could have been hurt because Jesus apparently ignored his suggestion, or he could have been crushed by the realization that it wasn't a very good idea, that he'd missed the point entirely. He could have said, "I'll never say another word. *Never.*" But he didn't. Instead, he was the one chosen to deliver the first gospel message that made 3,000 people ask what they should do about Jesus (Acts 2).

Misunderstanding was not Peter's only failure. He was also the man whose faith wavered as his eyes left Jesus when he stepped out of the boat to walk on the sea. He was the man who resorted to violence when the soldiers came to take Jesus away. He was the apostle who denied his beloved Master three times during Jesus' ordeal.

Peter is God's encouragement, his symbol of hope for all of us who sometimes fail. Martin Luther must have felt that when he wrote: "Whenever I look at Peter, my very heart leaps for joy. If I could paint a portrait of Peter, I would paint upon every hair of his head, 'I believe in forgiveness of sins.' "

Amazingly, God chooses to work through imperfect people. From the beginning of His Word to the end, He shows us that. I decided a long time ago not to be immobilized by failure and live out my life on a couch. I finally understood that the only people who don't sometimes fail are those who don't do anything. Peter was the only disciple who had the faith and adventurous spirit to get out of that boat. He was the one who at least did *something* when his Lord was being arrested. He was the one who went as far as the courtyard to see what happened to his master. Nevermind failure, he loved and trusted Jesus very much. So when Jesus rose from the dead, He told the women to go tell the disciples and *Peter* that He was risen. Especially Peter. He had a first gospel sermon to preach.

I'm so glad I "endured." If I hadn't, I would not be teaching English today, I would not be leading little children in worship, I would not be lecturing, I would not be singing, I would not be writing, I would not be growing to be more like Him. I would not be living.

So when the girls came home embarrassed out of their minds because they had done something stupid, we laughed. No matter how brutal. Even if Stacey tripped in the gym running around the floor at full speed. Even if she had practically tucked and rolled over three times, finally landing flat on her back in front of a bunch of senior boys sitting on the bleachers.

They've accepted their challenges now, unafraid of "failure." They've taught Sunday school classes when they didn't know how. They've spent their spring break working with the underprivileged in the inner-city of Atlanta. Stacey is planning a missions trip out of the country. Although so many of the things she'll be asked to do will be new to her, and although she doesn't know who else will be going, she's heading out anyway, unafraid of failure.

Maybe that's because she's seen me survive it; she's seen God use her dad and me when it seemed impossible. But more likely it's because she and her sister now shout in their hearts what God told the assembling army of Judah to shout: "Let the weak say, I am strong" (Joel 3:10). The girls know that because of Jesus, somehow that is true.

Chapter Eighteen

"He Loves His Church"

One Sunday after church, Stacey and I sat talking in our car in the parking lot of a local fast-food chain. While we waited for Tony and Leanne to get our dinner, Stacey told me about the waterskiing trip the youth group had gone on the day before. They had had a great time, and Stacey closed her account of the event by saying, "I want a boat when I grow up, Mom."

I don't know why I got so serious, but I did. I said, "That would be nice, Stace, but please never take your boat out on Sunday and miss church."

Her answer was just as serious. "I won't, Mama." I hope she will always say that.

She probably answered me so seriously because she knows

how important I think church and church attendance is. One thing we've taught the girls is to "gather together." Jesus said, "The love of most will grow cold" (Matt. 24:12). The first time I read that, I could hardly believe it. He said "love" (these were not people who didn't care much to begin with), and He said "most." That doesn't have to happen. It's entirely up to us. We can decide to, as John put it, "remain in Him" (I John 2:27). I'm convinced that one of the major ways we can remain in Him is to be devoted to the church.

God's people today must imitate those early followers of Jesus who "devoted themselves to the apostles' teaching and fellowship, to the breaking of bread and the prayers" (Acts 2:42, RSV). All these things — learning, fellowshiping and worshiping — are part of today's church, and thay have the potential to keep us strong. I know it's not the entire answer to "remaining in Christ," but it is an important part of it.

We have so much to learn about God and His Word and His will for our lives. The lessons and sermons we hear are important. They offset the lies the world often dumps on us and our children. That's one of the reasons why I took the kids to so many church services and activities, conferences, and camps. I took them any place they could be exposed to God's word. We need to constantly hear the truth it contains. It is a rich truth, able to continually show us new things. As we read and study a passage ourselves and then listen to what others have discovered within a passage, more and more is revealed to us.

I'm always puzzled when I see people who feel they have no need for study and regularly absent themselves from so many study opportunities. The Word never stops teaching us: it holds every answer, every comfort, every promise. It is wisdom and truth. It will do for us what all the self-help books, good as some are, cannot do. The Word, when we let it, will help us grow to be more like God, to be more one with God.

Breaking the "Bread of Life" is one way to "seek first the kingdom of God, and his righteousness" (Matt. 6:33). This was the one thing in life I did not want to neglect, because it would not only affect this life, but our eternal destiny. We could not let good things become bad because of a lack of balance. Too often, everything else in our lives takes precedence over Christ and His church. I never wanted spiritual things to be accidentally shoved to the perimeter of our hearts and mind. For I know that happens; Jesus said it would. For many people spiritual things will be forgotten altogether.

When we leave the world to worship, we do more than learn. We remember God. The whole world may not realize who God is, but many of us do, and we stand together and sing, "Holy, Holy, Holy, Lord God Almighty." As a family we've sung praise songs together for twenty years. Stacey was once asked to write a short paragraph about Sunday: "Sunday is one of my favorite days of the week. It's special because it's the day we go to church. Even though I (now) go to chapel during the week, I still love going to church on Sunday morning. It's the only time I get to worship with my family. Singing hymns with the family every Sunday morning will be one of the things I truly miss when I have to move on."

As we sing, we remember *whose* we are. Around the Lord's table, we remember *why*. We taught the girls to be jealous of this moment each week. Love is less likely to grow cold in the hearts of those who "remember," both individually and corporately.

We also taught the girls that attending church is important because of what we do for one another. Paul knew it: "Let us not give up meeting together, as some are in the habit of doing, but let us encourage one another" (Hebrews 10:25). A lady stopped me one evening at church and told me how glad it made her to see me and my family so faithful to the Lord's church. I thought that was a strange thing to say since we'd been attending there regularly for six years at the time, but I thanked her anyway.

As I thought about it, I realized that when Christians gather together, it just helps. Our presence witnesses. It's a statement repeated over and over again: "I believe. This is important to me. Everything else is subordinate to the Lord who has asked us to come together." That builds one another up. It is something children understand; something they never forget. When my mom and dad came to God when I was ten, they began a love relationship with Him that profoundly affected my life. Their lives utterly changed, and one thing they were committed to was being in God's house. Their attendance was not ritualistic or fanatic. It was a matter of priority. Since my dad was a railroad engineer, sometimes he was out of town on a run Wednesday evenings when our church had a mid-week service. My mom was a private secretary who worked long, hard hours and then came home to too many chores since we kids didn't help out enough. But always she put aside everything else, including her desire to rest, and packed the three of us up and took us to hear about God. Maybe sometimes we didn't even learn all that much, but whatever it was, it was more than we would have learned if we hadn't gone. And we surely learned a great deal from our mother's devotion.

Now, today, I have friends, who, not motivated by habit or obligation, are totally dedicated to the Lord's church. It is a faithfulness born of a deep love for Jesus, the head of the church. Our worship together encourages us and helps keep our hearts from growing cold.

Church, in its own special way, has bound our family together. Like Sunday mornings. When Leanne is living forty-five minutes away from us after she marries Scott this summer, and when Stacey is in Denver working for the summer, there are bound to be Sunday mornings I shall look out at the congregation from the choir loft where I often sit, and "see" them there — even when they are not.

See them singing. See them laying their heads over on their dad's shoulder while they listen to the preacher. See them getting my attention to try and make me laugh, or at least smile. See them take communion together. One morning the choir sang a special song during communion called "Shalom." The tender song with its gentle melody contained the words "Peace, I leave with you." As I thought about this promise of Jesus and sang the word Shalom slowly and softly over and over again, I looked out at the girls, who were taking communion reverently, and fought to keep my brimming tears from falling. It is a glorious thing for this mother to know that on Sunday mornings during this unique summer of our lives, the girls will share a bond with Tony and me. Each of us will be in some church, sharing the Lord's Supper, a love for God, and the peace that love brings.

We have made so many memories. One night not long ago, Stacey, Tony and I sat together during a Wednesday night class. We were right in the middle of an overview of the Bible and happened to be in Nehemiah. I found a verse in chapter two that I really liked and nudged Stacey. I whispered to her that I wanted that verse for my epitaph, for it surely was a truth that represented my life: "The gracious hand of my God was upon me" (2:8). She nodded; we both loved it. Although Tony shot us a look of reproach for talking in class, we thought the exchange worth it. Later I heard Stacey use the text in a lovely devotion she gave. We learned and shared something on that seemingly insignificant Wednesday night in the Lord's house. Tony really liked the verse, too, and I do hope he has it chiseled on my tombstone.

The girls have memorized a lot of scripture verses through the years, but I can only recall one that I personally asked them to memorize. All three of us memorized it, which was a challenge for me, given my memory problem. It was Phil. 4:8: "Finally, brothers, whatever is true, whatever is noble, whatever is right, whatever is pure, whatever is lovely, whatever is admirable — if anything is excellent or praiseworthy — think about such things."

That is one of the great lessons of life. We are what we think; we become what we dwell on. That is why Tony and I were so concerned about exposing the girls to spiritual things. We took them a lot of places to hear about God, not just church. For instance, even on a school night I took them with me one night to a women's conference to hear a speech by a seventy-year-old black lady who was a member of an exciting missions organization. I wanted them to hear her, because she is a woman who has "walked by faith." I felt like the girls would learn more about God by listening to her, and we were not disappointed.

She told about a time when her family decided to go to the slums of Pittsburgh, Pennsylvania, to minister. Although her husband had a job and they received a little support, existence was still precarious, partly because they couldn't stand to see their neighbors without necessities. They bought milk for babies and did whatever else they could until they had no more to give.

On one occasion they completely ran out of food and money and did not expect any for a long time. On Sunday afternoon they called a family meeting and told their children they had only enough food to last until breakfast Monday morning. They shared this concern with their children so that they would know that God hears and answers prayer.

After they prayed, this trusting woman called her daughter to the kitchen to scrub cabinets and clean the refrigerator so they'd be ready for whatever God supplied. She laughed and told her daughter that it would be easy to clean since nothing was in the way.

The next morning, after fixing their "last" breakfast, she sent the kids off to school, telling them not to worry. They hadn't been gone long when she and her husband saw a car drive up to the apartment building. The driver seemed to be looking for something. He got out and made his way to the family's front door.

The man had travelled many miles, he explained. His church had had supplies for them for a month, but he had been very busy and kept putting the trip off. But the night before, he became so "bothered" that he could not delay coming any longer. He took the day off to bring the month-old supplies, plus money and fresh meat the church had collected the night before.

The speaker said she shouted, "Hallelujah!" Then she grabbed the man's hand, rushed him into the kitchen, threw open the doors and showed him the bare shelves. And they cried. Faith increased for them that day. It increased for us that night.

Camp was another thing that exposed the girls to spiritual truths in a big dose. Some years they went to as many as three different church camps. We felt it was worth it. The first year we sent them to camp, they hated it. They were homesick and hot. I thought it too bad that they didn't have a perfect week, but it never occurred to me not to send them back the next summer. I had a friend who seemed surprised by that. She asked me how I got them to go. Now it was my turn to be surprised. I looked at her and said, "They were only nine and ten!" Actually, as bad as the girls hated camp that first year, it hardly entered their minds to try to boycott the next year. They knew I thought it was good for them, and that was that. I made them do a lot of things that didn't thrill them at the time. Yes, night after night they brushed their teeth. Day after day, I sent them off to school. What they learned in camp was as important to me as those things.

The second year they came home from camp happy as could be. And each year after that it was a highlight of their summer. A lot of times, because I was a member of a camp faculty, the three of us went together. One year we went to a large camp held on a state university campus, and the girls stayed with me in the apartment I was furnished.

One afternoon after classes were over and before dinner and the evening sessions began, we sat relaxing in the apartment together. Something we had heard made us start talking about Heaven. I told the girls that I was not sure what Heaven would be like, but I thought the gold streets might be figurative, that we could not imagine the glory that we would actually see. I also told them I didn't think I'd be wearin' a halo, strummin' a harp, and sittin' on clouds.

Then the conversation took a slight turn, something of a serious one, although the tone was still light. We speculated on what each of the three of us would do when we saw God. To do this, we imagined He would be sitting on His throne. Leanne decided she would run up to Him and jump on His lap, hug Him tightly (naturally) and say, "I love you, love you, love you."

Stacey was appalled by such familiarity. That was certainly not what she would do. She would just stand there and smile. Then she would walk up to Him, and from a short but appropriate distance, reach out her hand and shake His while saying, "Hello, Sir. I am *so* glad to see you."

Then it was my turn to imagine what I would do. I did not have to ponder it long. I told them I would stand before Him, look into His eyes, and then bury my face in my hands and sob.

Camp made us think of such things.

The girls were not the kind to get up in front of people at camp. They were the kind to make decisions in their hearts. But they made plenty of decisions at camp. Life-long ones.

On the closing night of camp when Stacey was a junior, I sat with the girls, although several of their friends sat between us. As I was praying and meditating during the lengthy and fairly emotional invitation time, the girl next to me tapped me on the shoulder and gave me a folded sheet of paper. As I opened it, I had no idea this would be one of the sweetest moments of my life:

Mom,
I really thought about going forward tonight. I didn't because I didn't know what to say. I do know I'm going to Bible college. I don't want you to think that I'm ignoring God in my future

plans, and forgetting about full-time Christian service. I've been thinking a lot about that lately. Maybe I'll run off and be a missionary, I don't know. I want you to know I've been praying about what God wants me to do with my life. I really want to do what He wants (I wonder who taught me that?) Well, I just thought this might make you happy. I love you.

Stacey

She had made me enormously happy. So did Leanne one night during her senior year. On a Wednesday might she asked me if I would ride to church with her in her car. She had a tape with a song on it that she listened to over and over again and just loved. She wanted me to hear it; she thought I would love it, too. The song is called "Lord of All." In the verses it talks about Jesus being Lord of everything, things we might not think about every day. Like "the power not to sin." He is Lord of "a peace that we can draw with ev'ry breath" and "of provision for each need in life and death." He is Lord of all — "the turnings of the seasons and the earth" and "the love that purchased man a second birth." After each verse was a beautiful refrain. Maybe we love that song so much because the refrain is the refrain of our hearts: "You have always been and always will be Lord of All."